GERMANY ATLAS ROAD MAP 2025

NAVIGATE GERMANY LIKE A LOCAL WITH DETAILED ROAD MAPS, HIDDEN GEMS, AND CULTURAL INSIGHTS FOR 2025 TRAVELERS

JOHANN MAXWELL

Copyright © 2025 by JOHANN MAXWELL

All rights reserved.

No part of this publication may be reproduced, distributed or transmitted in any form or by any means, including photocopying, recording or other electronic or mechanical methods, without the prior written permission of the publisher, except in the case of brief quotations embodied in critical reviews and certain other noncommercial uses permitted by copyright law.

Table of Contents

Introduction 10
    Overview of Germany Geography, Culture and Major Attractions 10
    Why Germany Is a Must-Visit Destination for Travelers in 2025 . 11
    The Importance of Having a Detailed Atlas and Road Map for Navigating Germany 12
    Key Insights on Traveling by Car, Public Transport and Bike 13
    Tips for First-Time Visitors to Germany 14

Chapter 1 16
    Preparing for Your Journey with Essential Travel Documents 16
    Visa and Entry Requirements for International Travelers 16
    Currency and Money Management 17
    Packing for Germany 18
    Health and Safety 20
    Cultural Etiquette 21

Chapter 2 24
    Driving in Germany 24
    Overview of German Road Infrastructure 24
    Traffic Laws and Regulations 25
    Toll Roads and Fuel in Germany 26
    Car Rental in Germany 28
    Eco-Friendly Travel 29

Chapter 3 30
    The Best Routes Across Germany 30

- Iconic Road Trips 30
- Scenic Byways of Germany 32
- Major Cities and Regional Highlights 33

Chapter 4 68
- Navigating Germany's Regions 68
- Northern Germany 68
- Southern Germany 70
- Eastern Germany 71
- Western Germany 73

Chapter 5 102
- Major Highways and Road Networks 102
- Autobahns Germany's World-Famous Highways 102
- Motorways and Federal Roads 104
- Navigational Tools 105

Chapter 6 108
- Regional Driving Laws and Special Considerations 108
- Environmental Zones (Low Emission Zones) 108
- Winter Driving 109
- Roundabouts and Traffic Circles 110
- Pedestrian Zones 112

Chapter 7 114
- Accommodations and Places to Stay 114
- Hotel Options 114
- Camping and Caravanning 116
- Hostels and Guesthouses 117

Local Cuisine and Food Stops..118

Food Festivals 119

Chapter 8..132

Final Tips for a Safe and Enjoyable Road Trip.........................132

Road Trip Safety 132

Travel Etiquette...133

Sustainability on the Road..134

Service Areas on the Autobahn...135

Scenic Stops and Hidden Gems 136

Chapter 9..142

Conclusion...142

Final Reflections, Road Wisdom & Travel Takeaways.............142

A Recap of Your Road Trip Playbook.......................................142

Final Travel Etiquette & Safety Tips 144

Final Words of Encouragement..146

Bremen
Hanover
Potsdam
Magdebur
Bielefeld
Dortmund
Kassel
Germany
eldorf
ogne
Frankfurt am Main
Mannheim
Nuremberg

Munich

Cologne

Berlin

Introduction

Overview of Germany Geography, Culture and Major Attractions

Germany isn't just a country you pass through; it's a destination you experience. It's a land where centuries-old castles perch on hillsides, high speed trains glide through valleys and forested trails can unexpectedly lead to the best slice of cake you have ever had. Nestled in the heart of Europe, Germany is a crossroads of history, modern innovation, and natural splendor.

Let's begin with geography because once you understand the physical shape of Germany, you start to realize why it's such an adventure-rich country. Stretching from the alpine peaks of the south to the flat, breezy north coasts, Germany covers nearly 138,000 square miles (about 357,000 square kilometers). It borders nine countries Denmark, Poland, the Czech Republic, Austria, Switzerland, France, Luxembourg, Belgium, and the Netherlands, making it one of Europe's most central and accessible countries.

The terrain is diverse: you have got the Alps in Bavaria, the Black Forest's dense woodlands, the sprawling plains of Saxony-Anhalt, and the Rhine River that has inspired poets and painters alike. The North Sea and Baltic coasts up north are a world away from the storybook villages of the south, yet both offer something unforgettable.

But Germany isn't just about what you see. It's about what you feel when you walk through the remnants of the Berlin Wall, stand before the mighty Cologne Cathedral, or sip Riesling while overlooking a vineyard-cloaked valley.

Germany's culture is rich, layered, and regionally distinct. In Bavaria, you'll hear "Grüß Gott" instead of Hallo, and beer isn't just a drink, it's a tradition. In Berlin, street art, underground music, and contemporary galleries thrive alongside war memorials and historical ruins. And in Saxony, opera houses sit proudly beside medieval towns.

Art, music, and literature have flourished here for centuries. Think of Beethoven, Bach, and Goethe, all German. Yet it's also a country where engineering meets design, home to BMW, Mercedes-Benz, and Porsche. Even the trains are a testament to German efficiency, arriving (mostly) on the dot.

Now, what about attractions?

Let's name a few essentials:

Berlin's Brandenburg Gate and Museum Island

Neuschwanstein Castle (you know the one that inspired Disney's castle?)

Oktoberfest in Munich

Cologne Cathedral—a Gothic marvel

The Romantic Road—a scenic route of half-timbered villages and castles

The Berlin Wall Memorial and Checkpoint Charlie

Heidelberg's Old Town

The Elbe Sandstone Mountains in Saxon Switzerland National Park

Whether you're into history, beer, art, nature, or perhaps all of the above, Germany gives you more than you expect, often when you least expect it.

Why Germany Is a Must-Visit Destination for Travelers in 2025

Travel trends are changing. In 2025, travelers aren't just chasing sunshine and sea; they want depth, cultural experiences, and well-connected journeys that offer both variety and value. Germany checks all those boxes.

Here's why Germany deserves your attention this year

1. Safe, Clean, and Traveler-Friendly

Germany consistently ranks among the safest countries to travel in Europe. Its cities are well-maintained, public services are reliable, and locals, though sometimes perceived as reserved, are immensely helpful once you break the ice.

2. Effortless Connections

Whether you're landing in Frankfurt, flying into Berlin, or arriving via rail from Paris, Germany is incredibly accessible. The Deutsche Bahn rail system, one of Europe's most efficient networks, connects nearly every corner of the country. Add to that a network of autobahns (yes, with no speed limit in certain zones) and cycling routes, and you've got seamless travel.

3. Balance of Urban and Natural Escapes

Berlin, Hamburg, and Munich are bustling metropolises with vibrant nightlife and a strong sense of identity. But just 30 minutes out, you could be walking beside a vineyard, cycling through a nature reserve, or exploring a UNESCO-listed monastery.

4. Cultural Renaissance

Post-pandemic, Germany has seen a revival in local arts, music festivals, and food culture. Markets are flourishing, and small towns are attracting more attention for their authenticity and charm.

5. Sustainability-First Travel

In 2025, Germany will continue to push forward on its environmental agenda. From eco-hotels to electric vehicle infrastructure and green-certified tour operators, it's easier than ever to travel consciously.

The Importance of Having a Detailed Atlas and Road Map for Navigating Germany

In an era of GPS apps and real-time digital maps, you might wonder: Why carry an atlas?

The answer is simple: a well-planned road trip starts on paper.

A physical atlas offers a big-picture perspective you just can't get from a five-inch screen. You can trace the entire route from the North Sea to the Bavarian Alps, find detours and hidden byways, or spot a small town you never knew existed but will fall in love with.

Here's why a detailed road map is still your best companion

Offline Security: Whether you're deep in the Black Forest or halfway across the Alps, the signal can and will drop. Paper never fails you.

Uncovering Hidden Routes: GPS typically guides you to the fastest way. Atlases highlight scenic roads, rest areas, and cultural sites you'd otherwise miss.

Better Planning: You'll understand distances, elevation, terrain, and how regions connect more clearly.

Visual Memory: There's something tactile and grounding about following your finger across a real map. You remember where you've been and where you're headed.

This book is designed to act as both a road companion and a cultural navigator, a resource that helps you plan not just where to go, but how to make each journey meaningful.

Key Insights on Traveling by Car, Public Transport and Bike

Germany offers a unique blend of travel modes, and the best trips often combine them.

By Car

Driving in Germany is pure joy, especially on the Autobahn. The roads are well-maintained, the signage is clear, and scenic routes abound. From the winding roads of the Moselle Valley to the mountain highways of Bavaria, having your own car means freedom and flexibility.

You'll be able to

Visit small villages that train the skipper.

Take your time at hidden scenic spots.

Pack without limits (no worrying about luggage weight)

But remember: you'll need to understand parking systems, environmental zones (Umweltzones), and how to read local traffic signs, which this book will guide you through in detail.

By Train

Germany's railway network is second to none. The InterCity Express (ICE) trains connect major cities like Munich, Berlin, and Hamburg at speeds up to 300 km/h. Regional trains (RE and RB) cover smaller towns and rural areas.

Benefits of train travel:

No stress about parking or road rules

Environmentally friendly

Excellent for solo or first-time travelers

By Bike

Germany is a cycling nation with more than 70,000 kilometers of well-marked bike paths. Whether it's a weekend tour along the Danube River or a short ride through Berlin Tiergarten, the country is remarkably bike-friendly.

Cities like Münster, Freiburg, and Leipzig have integrated cycling into their daily life, while rural routes offer paths through vineyards, lakesides, and castle-dotted hills.

Cycling allows you to slow down, connect with locals, and feel the rhythm of the landscape.

Tips for First-Time Visitors to Germany

If you've never been to Germany before, welcome, you're about to embark on one of the most enriching, diverse, and enjoyable journeys in Europe. But as with any travel experience, a few insights can make all the difference.

1. Cash Still Counts

Carry Cash and a Credit Card although credit cards are increasingly accepted, many small shops, restaurants, and cafes prefer cash. Having some euros on hand ensures smooth transactions.

2. Sunday Shutdown

On Sundays, most stores are closed. Plan accordingly, do your shopping on Saturday, and enjoy Sunday as the locals do: relaxing in a park or sipping coffee in a quiet café.

3. Mind the Quiet Hours

Germans value Ruhezeit (quiet time). This means noise is frowned upon from 10 PM to 6 AM and during lunchtime in some places. It's not just a courtesy it's the law in many residential areas.

4. Embrace Public Transportation

Germany boasts an efficient and reliable public transport system, including trains, trams, buses, and subways. Purchasing a travel pass or a regional transportation card can save money and make exploring cities like Berlin, Munich, and Hamburg more convenient.

5. Learn Basic German Phrases

While many Germans speak English, especially in cities, learning simple greetings and polite phrases like "Hallo" (Hello), "Danke" (Thank you), and "Bitte" (Please) can enhance your interactions and show respect for the local culture.

6. Be Mindful of Recycling and Waste Separation

Germany is known for its environmental consciousness. Pay attention to recycling symbols and disposal instructions to participate respectfully.

8. Explore Beyond Major Cities

While cities like Berlin and Munich are must-visit destinations, consider exploring smaller towns and picturesque regions like the Romantic Road, the Black Forest, and the Rhine Valley for a more intimate experience of Germany's diverse landscape and history.

Think of this guide not just as a map, but as a key to places you've dreamed of and others you've never heard of but won't forget. Whether you're here to cruise the Romantic Road, sip a beer at Oktoberfest, or simply take a long way home through the Black Forest, Germany has layers worth peeling back slowly.

So buckle up. Your journey across one of Europe's most fascinating, diverse, and welcoming countries is about to begin.

Chapter 1

Preparing for Your Journey with Essential Travel Documents

Before you daydream about strolling through a Bavarian village or cruising down the Autobahn, let's get the paperwork in order. Germany is known for its efficiency, and having well-organized travel documents will help you match that standard. Missing even one can derail your trip before it begins.

Visa and Entry Requirements for International Travelers

Germany is a member of the Schengen Area, a group of European countries with standardized border control policies. This means that once you're in, you can travel freely between other Schengen countries no border checks.

Here's what you need to know

1. Citizens from the EU/EEA and Switzerland: No visa needed. You just need a valid national ID card or passport.

2. USA, Canada, UK, Australia, New Zealand, Japan, South Korea and several others: You can enter Germany without a visa for tourism or business purposes for up to 90 days within 180 days.

3. Other countries: You will need a Schengen Visa. This is typically a short-stay visa that allows you to visit for up to 90 days. It must be applied for at the German embassy or consulate in your home country.

In 2025, the ETIAS (European Travel Information and Authorization System) may be in effect. This is not a visa, but a mandatory pre-travel authorization for travelers from visa-exempt countries. It's quick to apply online, and approval is usually fast.

Tip: Always check the latest visa rules on the German Federal Foreign Office website before traveling. Rules can change unexpectedly.

Travel Insurance Recommendations

Travel insurance isn't a luxury; it's a must. Whether it's a missed flight, stolen bag, or medical emergency, the right policy can save your trip (and your wallet).

What to look for in a travel insurance plan

Medical coverage (a minimum of €30,000 is required for Schengen visa holders)

Emergency evacuation

Trip cancellation/interruption

COVID-19-related coverage (still worth checking in 2025)

Some of the most reputable international travel insurers include Allianz Travel, World Nomads, AXA, and Safety Wing.

Required Documents for Car Rental in Germany

Planning to drive through the countryside? Fantastic idea but makes sure you have these:

A valid driver's license: If you're from the EU or EEA, your national license works. Travelers from outside the EU (like the US or Canada) should carry an International Driving Permit (IDP) in addition to their home license.

Passport

Credit card (for the security deposit)

Note: Rental companies may require drivers to be at least 21 years old, with one year of driving experience. Some high-end car rentals may set the minimum age at 25.

Currency and Money Management

Germany uses the Euro (EUR €). It's one of the most stable and widely used currencies in the world, and while Germany is a digital powerhouse, cash is still king in many parts of daily life.

Overview of the Euro and Payment Methods

Bills: €5, €10, €20, €50, €100, €200, €500 (though €200 and €500 bills are rare)

Coins: 1, 2, 5, 10, 20, 50 cents, €1, and €2

Many businesses, especially bakeries, corner cafés, and traditional markets, prefer cash, especially for small purchases.

Larger stores, restaurants, and hotels will usually accept Visa and Mastercard, but American Express is less common

Tips for Exchanging Currency and Using ATMs

1. Avoid exchanging cash at airports or hotels; the rates are usually poor.

2. Use ATMs (Bankautomat) for the best exchange rates. Stick to ATMs located outside or inside major banks, not generic or third-party machines in tourist areas.

3. Many German ATMs ask if you want to convert to your home currency decline this offer and choose to be charged in Euros for better exchange rates.

4. Credit and debit cards with contactless features are widely accepted in urban areas.

5. Apple Pay and Google Pay are increasingly popular in cities, especially in larger retail stores, restaurants, and public transport systems.

However, don't rely on mobile payment alone always carry some cash, especially in smaller towns and rural areas.

Packing for Germany

Packing smartly can make or break your comfort on the road. Germany's climate is as varied as its landscape, so what you pack depends heavily on the season and regions you're visiting.

What to Bring Based on the Season

1. Winter (December–February)

Thermal layers, waterproof boots, insulated coat

Gloves, a scarf, and a hat, especially in Bavaria and the Alps

Warm sleepwear for older guests

2. Spring (March-May)

Lightweight jacket or raincoat

Umbrella (April can be rainy)

Comfortable walking shoes (some trails may be muddy)

3. Summer (June–August)

T-shirts, breathable pants, or shorts

Sun hat, sunglasses, and sunscreen

Swimsuit for lakes and spas

4. Autumn (September–November):

Warm layers, sturdy shoes

Waterproof jacket (fall can be wet)

Neutral-colored outfits for wine festivals or city tours

Guidelines for Packing Light vs. Packing for Long Stays

Packing Light (1–2 weeks)

Capsule wardrobe (mix-and-match basics)

Reusable tote for shopping

Foldable daypack or crossbody bag

Packing for Long Stays (3+ weeks)

Travel laundry kit or plan for local laundromats

More than one pair of durable shoes

Compact travel steamer or wrinkle-release spray

Travel Essentials to Remember

Power adapter (Germany uses type C and F plugs, 230V)

Portable charger/power bank

Unlocked phone with eSIM or local SIM option

Language guidebook or translation app

Copy of passport and travel documents (digital and printed)

Reusable water bottle

Travel-sized toiletries

Health and Safety

Germany ranks high in health and hygiene standards, but a few precautions can make your trip smoother and safer.

Travel Vaccinations and Health Precautions

No special vaccinations are required for entry into Germany from most countries, but it's wise to be up to date on:

- Routine vaccines (MMR, DTP, Hepatitis A & B)
- Seasonal flu shot
- COVID-19 vaccinations and boosters
- Mosquito-borne diseases and other tropical illnesses are not a concern.

Tip: If you're hiking or camping, check for tick-borne encephalitis risks in forested areas (e.g., Bavaria, Black Forest), and consider the vaccine if you'll be in rural areas long-term.

How to Handle Emergencies

Emergency Number (Police, Fire, Ambulance): 112

Non-Emergency Medical Help: 116 117

Pharmacies (Apotheke) are well-marked by a red "A" sign. Pharmacists are knowledgeable and often speak English.

In major cities, hospitals, Krankenhaus and clinics are of a very high standard.

Health Insurance Options for Travelers

EU citizens should carry their European Health Insurance Card (EHIC) for access to German healthcare.

Non-EU travelers should carry proof of international travel insurance that covers medical treatment in Germany. Hospitals will treat you regardless, but without insurance, you may face large bills.

Cultural Etiquette

Understanding the social norms in Germany not only avoids awkward situations but also shows respect. Germans appreciate thoughtful, polite behavior.

Language Tips (Common Phrases in German)

Even if many Germans speak English, learning a few key phrases will go a long way:

Hallo! – Hello

Guten Tag! – Good day

Tschüss! – Bye

Bitte – Please / You're welcome

Danke – Thank you

Entschuldigung – Excuse me

Sprechen Sie Englisch? – Do you speak English?

Wo ist...? – Where is...?

Die Rechnung, bitte. – The bill, please

Social Customs, Tipping, and Behavior Norms

Germans value punctuality. Arrive on time for tours, trains, and appointments.

Greet with a handshake, especially in formal settings

Tipping (Trinkgeld) is appreciated, but not excessive, rounding up or adding 5–10% in restaurants is customary.

Quiet and order are valued in public spaces. Keep phone calls low and don't talk loudly on trains or in restaurants.

Don't cross the street at a red pedestrian light, even if there's no traffic. It's frowned upon and sometimes fined.

Local Food Etiquette and Drinking Culture

In restaurants, waiting to be seated is common, especially in fine dining.

Bread is often served without butter unless you ask.

Sharing tables (especially in beer gardens) is normal; just ask if the seat is free.

When toasting, make eye contact with each person and say "Prost!"

Beer is served in standard sizes depending on the region; don't expect a giant stein everywhere.

Tap water isn't automatically served; you'll need to request it.

Traveling to Germany in 2025 is an exciting adventure filled with historic cities, lush countryside and efficient infrastructure, but it all begins with being well-prepared. From securing your visa and renting a car to understanding public customs and currency

When you pack well, plan smart, and know a few key local norms, you're not just visiting, you're engaging. And that's the real beauty of travel.

Chapter 2

Driving in Germany

Driving in Germany offers one of the most thrilling, efficient, and picturesque experiences for travelers. With world famous autobahns charming countryside routes, and cities that blend historic character with modern efficiency, the country is perfectly suited for road travel. Whether you're a seasoned driver or exploring the open roads of Germany for the first time, understanding how the road network functions, the laws that govern it and the available options for car rentals is essential for a smooth and enjoyable journey.

Overview of German Road Infrastructure

Autobahns: What You Need to Know About High-Speed Highways

The German autobahn is legendary among drivers around the world. Known for stretches with no general speed limit, these highways are engineered for safety and efficiency. However, while certain segments allow drivers to travel at unrestricted speeds, many parts do have posted limits, especially near cities, construction zones, or accident-prone areas.

Autobahns are denoted by an "A" followed by a number, such as A9 or A3. These multi-lane roads are designed for high-speed travel and are well-maintained. Traffic typically flows smoothly, and there are frequent rest stops (called Raststätten or Autohöfe) offering services like restaurants, fuel, and restrooms.

Key autobahn etiquette includes:

Stay Right: Always keep to the right unless overtaking.

No Passing on the Right: It's illegal to overtake a car on the right on the Autobahn.

Observe Recommended Speeds: While not mandatory, the advisory speed (Richtgeschwindigkeit) is 130 km/h (about 81 mph).

Local Roads, Rural Routes, and Scenic Byways

Beyond the autobahns, germany offers an extensive network of Bundesstraßen (federal highways), Landesstraßen (state roads), and Kreisstraßen (district roads). These are well-signed and can take you through charming villages, historic town and breathtaking landscapes, particularly in regions like Bavaria, the Black Forest, and the Rhine Valley.

Scenic routes like the Romantic Road (Romantische Straße) or Wine Route (Weinstraße) are ideal for travelers wanting to combine cultural discovery with the joy of driving. These routes are perfect for slower-paced exploration.

City Driving vs. Countryside Driving

Driving in German cities can be challenging for those unfamiliar with narrow lanes, cyclists, and pedestrian zones. Most cities also have Umweltzonen (environmental zones) where only vehicles with a special emissions sticker (Feinstaubplakette) are allowed.

.

Traffic Laws and Regulations

Speed Limits and Road Signs Explained

Speed limits in Germany are posted and enforced. Standard speed limits include:

Urban areas (innerorts): 50 km/h (31 mph)

Rural roads (außerorts): 100 km/h (62 mph)

Autobahn: No general limit, but 130 km/h is recommended unless otherwise posted

German road signs are mostly pictographic, with triangular warning signs and circular regulatory signs. Key ones include:

The red circle with a number: Speed limit

A blue sign with white arrows: Directional instructions or lanes

A white diamond with a yellow border: Priority road

Triangle with deer: Wildlife crossing area

Parking Regulations and Tips for City Parking

Parking in Germany varies widely by location

Parken verboten" signs indicate no parking zones.

Blue signs with a white "P" indicate official parking areas.

Park and Ride (P+R) lots near transit stations are cost-effective options.

Pay attention to painted curbs-yellow lines usually mean no parking. Most urban parking requires payment via ticket machines or mobile apps like Parkopedia or EasyPark.

Rules on Overtaking, Lane Discipline, and Use of Mobile Phones

Germany places high importance on lane discipline:

Always overtake on the left- it's illegal and dangerous to pass on the right.

Mobile phone use is prohibited unless using a hands-free device. Violations come with heavy fines.

Child Safety Seat Laws and Other Specific Vehicle Regulations

Children under 12 or 150 cm (4 ft 11 in) must use approved child restraint systems. Seats must meet the ECE R44/04 or i-Size standards. It's also mandatory to carry:

- A warning triangle
- Reflective safety vest
- First-aid kit
- Spare bulbs

Toll Roads and Fuel in Germany

Understanding the Toll Systems (Vignettes, Motorway Fees)

Germany is renowned for its extensive and efficient transportation network, which includes a well-maintained system of highways, or Autobahnen.

Travelers and commuters alike benefit from this infrastructure, though there are important considerations regarding tolls and fuel.

Toll Roads

While many sections of Germany's Autobahnen are free to use, certain routes, particularly those connecting to neighboring countries or passing through urban areas, may require toll payments. As of 2025, Germany has implemented a lorry toll system (Maut) for freight vehicles over 7.5 tonnes, which is levied based on distance traveled, vehicle emissions, and size. This system aims to promote environmentally friendly transportation and maintain road quality.

Fuel Prices, Fuel Stations, and Tips for Refueling

Fuel in Germany is relatively expensive compared to other countries. Gasoline (Benzin) and diesel (Diesel) are widely available, with premium grades often marked as "Super" or "Super Plus." Prices are typically per liter.

Fuel stations are plentiful and often open late, especially along highways. Most accept credit cards and offer self-service. Apps like Clever Tanken can help you find the best local prices.

Diesel vs. Petrol Cars and Hybrid/Electric Vehicle Options

Many rental cars in Germany are diesel-powered, known for fuel efficiency, especially for long-distance travel. However, diesel bans in some city centers for older vehicles exist, so check with your rental company.

Electric and hybrid options are becoming more popular, especially for eco-conscious travelers. Charging stations are increasing with networks like Ionity and EnBW covering major routes.

Tips for Travelers

- Always carry some cash or a card accepted by most fuel stations.
- Plan your refueling stops in advance, especially in rural areas where stations may be less frequent.

Car Rental in Germany

Exploring Germany by car offers travelers the ultimate flexibility to discover its diverse landscapes, historic cities, and scenic countryside at their own pace. Renting a car in Germany is a straightforward process, with numerous options available for visitors from around the world.

Rental Agencies and Availability

Major international car rental companies such as Hertz, Avis, Enterprise, and Europcar maintain a strong presence across the country. Additionally, local providers often offer competitive rates and personalized service. Most rental offices are located at airports, major train stations, and city centers, making access convenient for travelers.

Driving Requirements

To rent a car in Germany, drivers typically need to be at least 18 years old, though some companies may require a minimum age of 21 or 25. A valid driver's license from your home country is usually sufficient for short-term rentals, but an International Driving Permit (IDP) may be recommended or required for certain nationalities. It's advisable to carry your passport, driver's license, and rental agreement at all times.

Be sure to inspect the vehicle and take photos before and after the rental to avoid disputes.

Driving License Requirements and International Driving Permits

EU and EEA licenses are valid in Germany without restriction. For travelers from non-EU countries, many car rental agencies require an International Driving Permit (IDP) in addition to your home license, especially if it's not in Latin script.

Cost Considerations

Rental prices vary depending on the vehicle type, rental duration, and season. Additional costs may include insurance options, tolls, and fuel. Germany's fuel prices are generally competitive within Europe. Planning ahead and comparing offers can help secure the best deal.

Eco-Friendly Travel

Germany is leading in green transport infrastructure. Many rental agencies offer electric cars like the BMW i3, Volkswagen ID.4, or Tesla Model 3. Charging stations are widespread, especially in urban areas and along highways. App like Plugsurfing or ChargeMap can help you locate compatible charging stations, some of which are free.

Stay in Eco-Conscious Accommodations

Look for hotels, hostels, and guesthouses that prioritize sustainability. Many establishments participate in green certifications, implement energy-saving measures and support local sourcing. Staying in eco-friendly accommodations helps reduce your carbon footprint while supporting environmentally responsible businesses.

Sustainable Travel Tips for Road Trips in Germany

- Choose a fuel-efficient or electric car.
- Plan routes efficiently to reduce unnecessary driving
- Avoid idling and aggressive acceleration.
- Reuse water bottles and cut down on single-use plastics during your journey.

Green Driving Practices to Reduce Fuel Consumption

- Driving smart not only saves money but also reduces emissions:
- Maintain a steady speed cruise control helps on highways.
- Drive in the highest gear possible without over-revving
- Keep tires properly inflated.

Germany's roadways offer more than just a means to get from point A to point B; they are part of the travel experience. Whether you're zipping down the autobahn, meandering through wine country, or navigating city centers, understanding the nuances of German driving culture will enhance your trip. With careful planning, knowledge of traffic laws, and an openness to explore sustainably, driving in Germany can be one of the most enjoyable ways to see the country.

Chapter 3

The Best Routes Across Germany

Germany isn't just a country; it's a mosaic of history, culture, nature, and timeless charm. And there's no better way to experience it all than by hitting the road. This section explores the most iconic road trips Germany has to offer, from castle studded routes to scenic coastal highways and alpine adventures. Whether you're cruising past vineyards, navigating forested mountains or exploring vibrant cities these routes offer travelers an immersive and unforgettable driving experience.

Iconic Road Trips

The Romantic Road (Romantische Straße)

Stretching roughly 400 km 250 miles from Würzburg to Füssen, the Romantic Road is Germany's most famous scenic route. It captures the essence of old-world Germany's cobblestone streets, half-timbered houses, fortified walls, and majestic castles.

Highlights

1. Würzburg: Start with the Baroque beauty of the Würzburg Residence, a UNESCO World Heritage Site.

2. Rothenburg ob der Tauber: A perfectly preserved medieval town, don't miss the city walls and the Christmas Museum.

3. Dinkelsbühl and Nördlingen: Less crowded but just as charming, offering authentic Franconian architecture.

4. Neuschwanstein Castle: The road culminates at this iconic fairy-tale castle nestled in the Alps near Füssen.

5. Driving Tip: Allow at least 4–5 days to explore towns in depth. Avoid the summer crowds by traveling in late spring or early fall.

The German Wine Road (Deutsche Weinstraße)

Winding through Rhineland-Palatinate for approximately 85 km (53 miles), the German Wine Road is among the country's oldest tourist routes, renowned for its Riesling wines and charming villages.

Highlights

1. Bad Dürkheim: Known for hosting the world's largest wine barrel and an annual wine festival.

2. Neustadt an der Weinstraße: Home to romantic alleyways, local wine taverns, and scenic vineyards.

3. Deidesheim: A quaint wine growing town offering superb tastings and gourmet cuisine

4. Seasonal Tip: Visit in September or October to enjoy the grape harvest and vibrant wine festivals along the route.

The Black Forest High Road (Schwarzwaldhochstraße)

Germany's oldest scenic route, this 60 km (37-mile) drive runs from Baden-Baden to Freudenstadt, winding through the northern Black Forest. Towering fir trees, winding roads, and alpine vistas make it a spectacular journey.

Highlights

1. Baden-Baden: is famous for its thermal baths and luxury spas.

2. Mummelsee Lake: A mystical glacial lake with folklore tales.

3. Freudenstadt: A lively town with one of Germany's largest marketplaces.

4. Driving Tip: In winter check weather conditions snowfall can affect visibility and road accessibility.

The Baltic Sea Coast (Ostseeküstenstraße)

From Flensburg near the Danish border to Usedom Island, the coastal road takes you past seaside resorts, white-sand beaches, and UNESCO World Heritage towns.

Highlights

1. **Lübeck:** A medieval hanseatic city with its iconic Holstentor Gate and marzipan delights.

2. **Wismar and Stralsund:** Stunning Brick Gothic architecture and maritime history.

3. **Rügen Island:** Famous for the white chalk cliffs of Jasmund National Park.

4. **Summer Tip:** The Baltic Coast is a local favorite during July and August. Book accommodations early.

The German Alpine Road (Deutsche Alpenstraße)

Running from Lindau on Lake Constance to Berchtesgaden, this 450 km (280-mile) route threads through Bavaria's Alpine landscape. It's ideal for mountain lovers and those seeking Bavarian tradition and nature.

Highlights

1. **Oberammergau:** Known for its Passion play and fresco-painted houses.

2. **Garmisch-Partenkirchen:** A gateway to Zugspitze, Germany's highest mountain.

3. **Nationalpark Berchtesgaden:** Rugged peaks, the turquoise Königssee, and the infamous Eagle's Nest.

4. **Travel Note:** Suitable year-round, but ideal in late spring or early fall to avoid tourist rushes and winter weather.

Scenic Byways of Germany

Germany is renowned for its picturesque landscapes, charming villages, and historic routes that offer travelers an immersive experience into the country's diverse beauty. The scenic byways weave through lush forests, rolling hills, and majestic mountains, providing unforgettable journeys for explorers seeking both adventure and tranquility.

The Castle Road (Burgenstraße)

Spanning over 1,000 km (620 miles) from Mannheim to Prague, this route showcases Germany's romantic and imperial past through its impressive collection of castles and palaces.

Notable Stops

1. Heidelberg Castle: Overlooking the Neckar River with dramatic views.

2. The Moselle Valley Route: Following the winding Moselle River, this route showcases terraced vineyards, quaint villages, and historic ruins.

3. Rothenburg ob der Tauber: A medieval gem worth a second mention.

4. Nuremberg: Rich in imperial history and Gothic architecture.

The Fairy Tale Route (Deutsche Märchenstraße)

Running over 600 km (370 miles) from Hanau (the Brothers Grimm's birthplace) to Bremen, this magical road takes you through forests, medieval towns, and stories that inspired Snow White, Rapunzel, and Hansel and Gretel.

Charming Stops

Steinau: Home to the Grimm Brothers Museum.

Sababurg: The "Sleeping Beauty Castle" is surrounded by enchanted woods.

Hameln: The town of the Pied Piper legend.

Major Cities and Regional Highlights

1. Berlin A Driving Tour of the Capital's Icons

Drive from Alexanderplatz past the TV Tower to the Brandenburg Gate, and then loop around the Tiergarten and Reichstag.

Visit the East Side Gallery, take a detour through Kreuzberg, and drive along the Spree River for a mix of old and New Berlin.

Parking Tip: Use park-and-ride facilities and explore the center on foot or by bike.

2. Munich Touring the Historical Center and Parks

Begin at Marienplatz, cruise by the Residenz, then head towards the English Garden, one of the largest urban parks in Europe.

Visit Nymphenburg Palace, the BMW Museum, and the Olympic Park for a blend of royal and modern highlights.

Driving Tip: Avoid peak hours, traffic can be heavy around ring roads.

3. Frankfurt Modern Architecture and Historical Charm

Drive through the Banking District, then down to the Römerberg, the city's medieval heart.

Don't miss the Main Tower for skyline views and the Palmengarten for peaceful greenery.

Great day trips from Frankfurt include the Taunus Mountains or Heidelberg.

4. Hamburg Exploring the Port and Maritime Heritage

Start in the HafenCity, visit the iconic Elbphilharmonie, and tour the historic Speicherstadt (warehouse district).

Drive along the Elbe River, past St. Pauli, to the beachy Blankenese district.

Tip: The Old Elbe Tunnel allows cars and pedestrians to pass under the river an unusual experience.

5. Cologne Gothic Wonders and the Rhine River

The Cologne Cathedral dominates the skyline and is the perfect start.

Cruise down the Rhine Promenade, visit the Chocolate Museum, and explore Ehrenfeld for artsy vibes.

Whether you're cruising through Alpine landscapes, meandering along vineyard-covered hills, or navigating bustling cityscapes, Germany's network of scenic and cultural routes offers something for every kind of traveler. From legendary fairy tales to cutting-edge architecture, every journey tells a story, your story.

Würzburg

SCAN HERE

HOW TO USE QR CODE

- Open your phone's camera app or download scanner app from play store or apple store
- Point the camera at the QR code for a few seconds (no need to take a photo).
- A link should appear on the display, leading you to the location of the code

Füssen

SCAN HERE

HOW TO USE QR CODE

- Open your phone's camera app or download scanner app from play store or apple store
- Point the camera at the QR code for a few seconds (no need to take a photo).
- A link should appear on the display, leading you to the location of the code

Rothenburg ob der Tauber

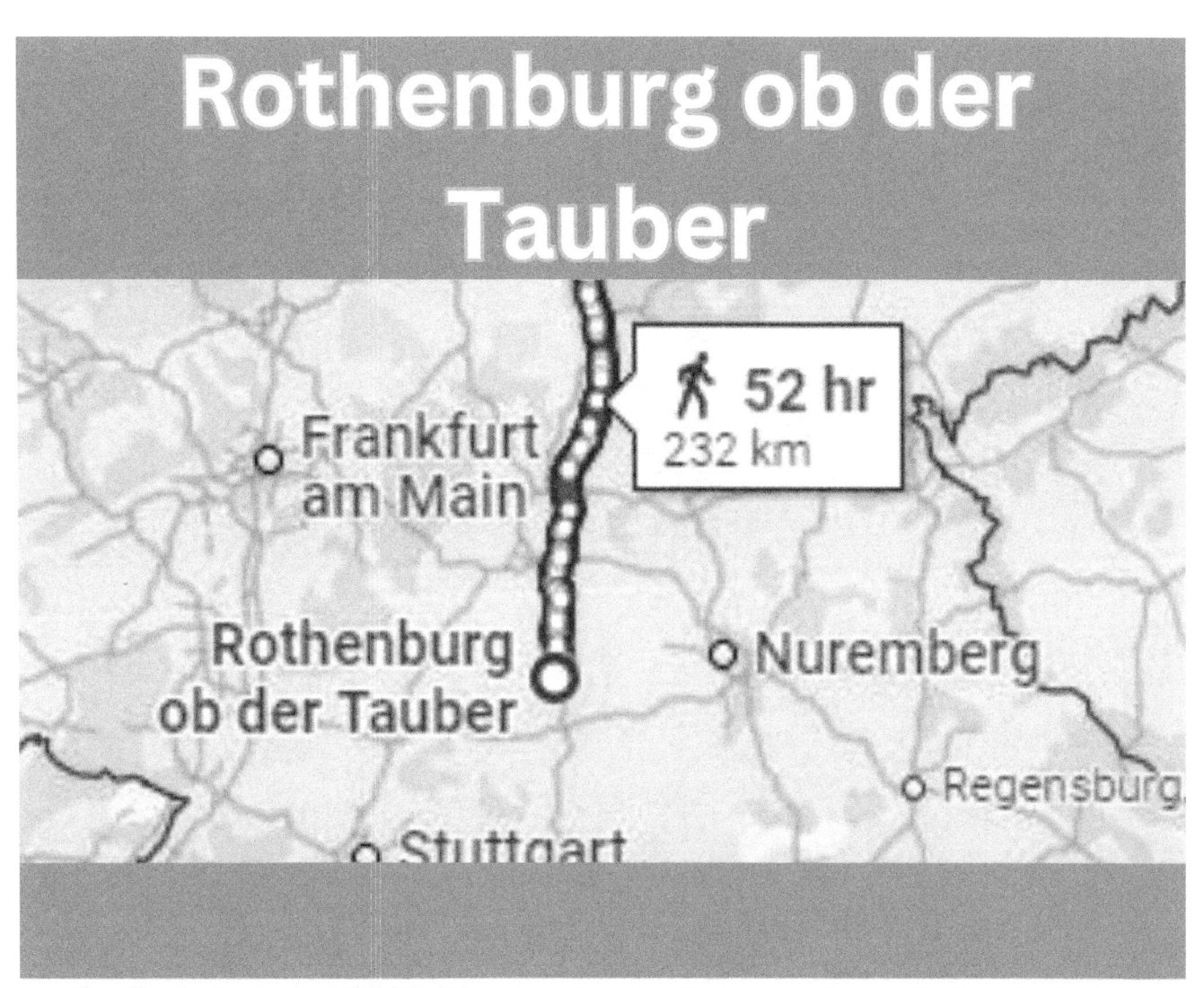

🚶 52 hr
232 km

SCAN HERE

HOW TO USE QR CODE

- Open your phone's camera app or download scanner app from play store or apple store
- Point the camera at the QR code for a few seconds (no need to take a photo).
- A link should appear on the display, leading you to the location of the code

Nördlingen

🚶 69 hr
301 km

SCAN HERE

HOW TO USE QR CODE

- Open your phone's camera app or download scanner app from play store or apple store
- Point the camera at the QR code for a few seconds (no need to take a photo).
- A link should appear on the display, leading you to the location of the code

Neuschwanstein Castle

Bad Dürkheim

🚶 65 hr
282 km

SCAN HERE

HOW TO USE QR CODE

- Open your phone's camera app or download scanner app from play store or apple store
- Point the camera at the QR code for a few seconds (no need to take a photo).
- A link should appear on the display, leading you to the location of the code

Neustadt

Deidesheim

SCAN HERE

HOW TO USE QR CODE

- Open your phone's camera app or download scanner app from play store or apple store
- Point the camera at the QR code for a few seconds (no need to take a photo).
- A link should appear on the display, leading you to the location of the code

Baden-Baden

SCAN HERE

HOW TO USE QR CODE

- Open your phone's camera app or download scanner app from play store or apple store
- Point the camera at the QR code for a few seconds (no need to take a photo).
- A link should appear on the display, leading you to the location of the code

Mummelsee

Freudenstadt

SCAN HERE

HOW TO USE QR CODE

- Open your phone's camera app or download scanner app from play store or apple store
- Point the camera at the QR code for a few seconds (no need to take a photo).
- A link should appear on the display, leading you to the location of the code

Flensburg

SCAN HERE

HOW TO USE QR CODE

- Open your phone's camera app or download scanner app from play store or apple store
- Point the camera at the QR code for a few seconds (no need to take a photo).
- A link should appear on the display, leading you to the location of the code

Lübeck

SCAN HERE

HOW TO USE QR CODE

- Open your phone's camera app or download scanner app from play store or apple store
- Point the camera at the QR code for a few seconds (no need to take a photo).
- A link should appear on the display, leading you to the location of the code

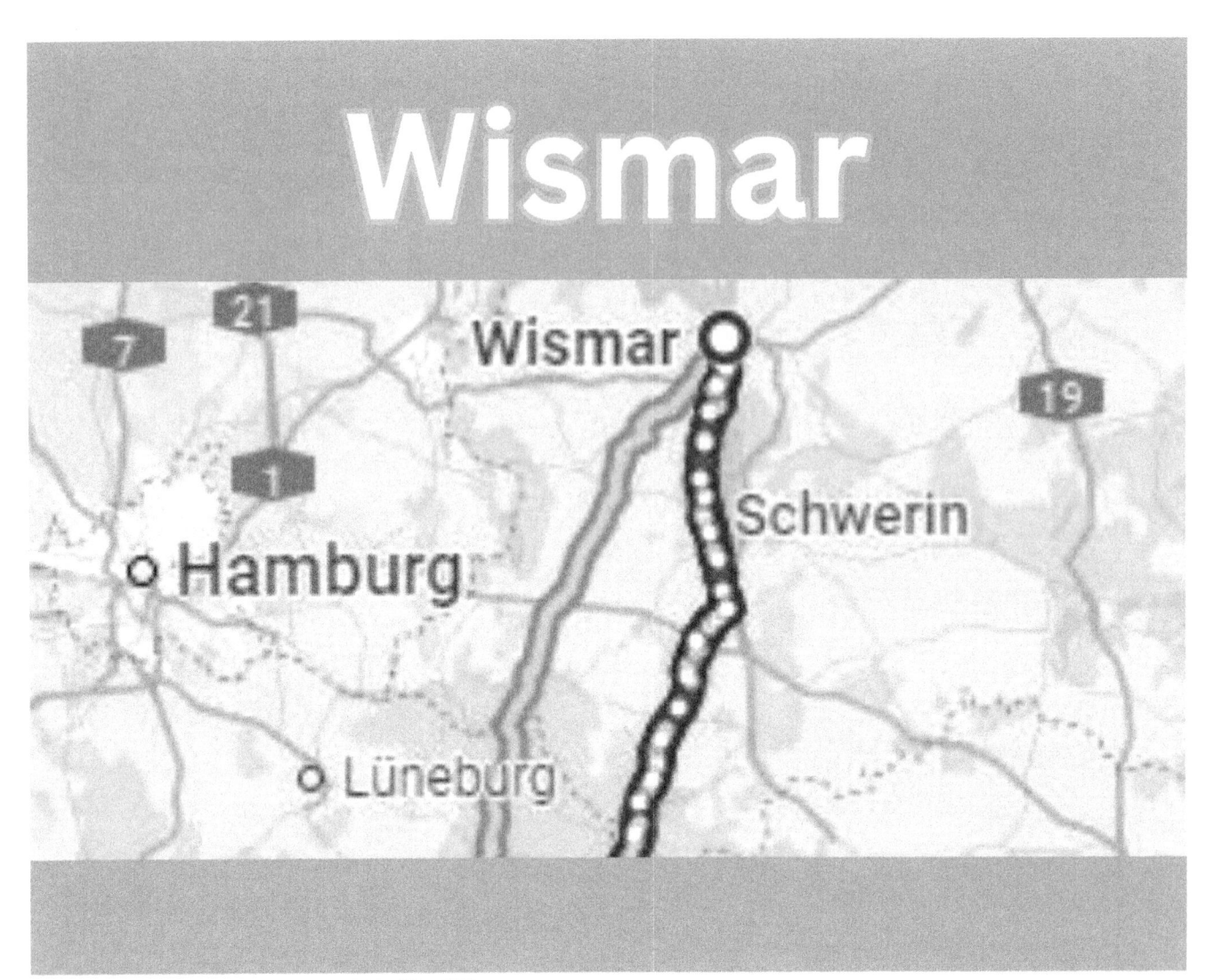

Wismar

SCAN HERE

HOW TO USE QR CODE

- Open your phone's camera app or download scanner app from play store or apple store
- Point the camera at the QR code for a few seconds (no need to take a photo).
- A link should appear on the display, leading you to the location of the code

Stralsund

SCAN HERE

HOW TO USE QR CODE

- Open your phone's camera app or download scanner app from play store or apple store
- Point the camera at the QR code for a few seconds (no need to take a photo).
- A link should appear on the display, leading you to the location of the code

Rügen Island

Garmisch-Partenkirchen

SCAN HERE

HOW TO USE QR CODE

- Open your phone's camera app or download scanner app from play store or apple store
- Point the camera at the QR code for a few seconds (no need to take a photo).
- A link should appear on the display, leading you to the location of the code

Nationalpark Berchtesgaden

Heidelberg Castle

Nuremberg

SCAN HERE

HOW TO USE QR CODE

- Open your phone's camera app or download scanner app from play store or apple store
- Point the camera at the QR code for a few seconds (no need to take a photo).
- A link should appear on the display, leading you to the location of the code

Sababurg

Hamelin

🚶 **34 hr**
149 km

SCAN HERE

HOW TO USE QR CODE

- Open your phone's camera app or download scanner app from play store or apple store
- Point the camera at the QR code for a few seconds (no need to take a photo).
- A link should appear on the display, leading you to the location of the code

Berlin

SCAN HERE

HOW TO USE QR CODE

- Open your phone's camera app or download scanner app from play store or apple store
- Point the camera at the QR code for a few seconds (no need to take a photo).
- A link should appear on the display, leading you to the location of the code

Alexanderplatz

Brandenburg Gate

Munich

SCAN HERE

HOW TO USE QR CODE

- Open your phone's camera app or download scanner app from play store or apple store
- Point the camera at the QR code for a few seconds (no need to take a photo).
- A link should appear on the display, leading you to the location of the code

Marienplatz

Nymphenburg Palace

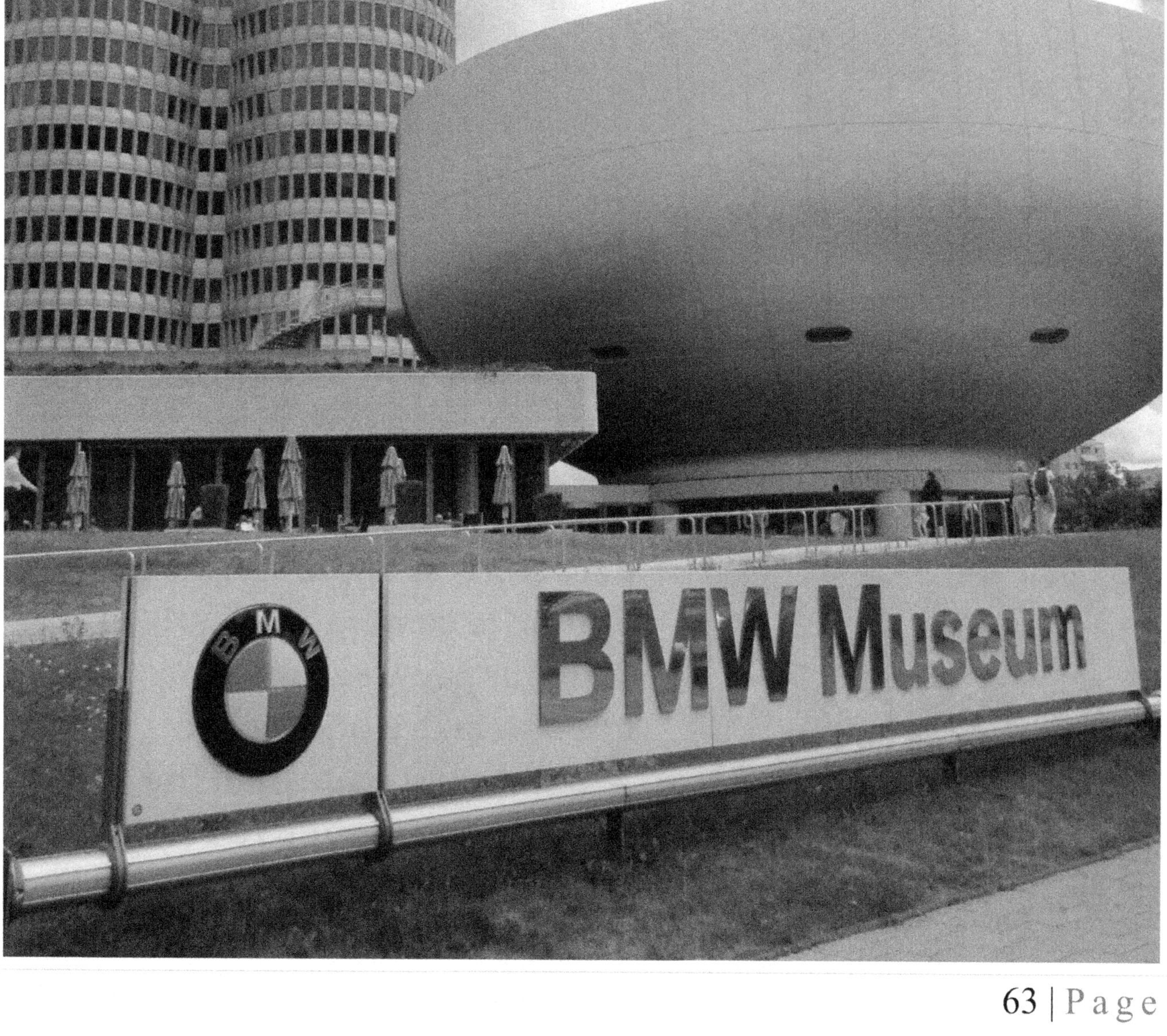
BMW
BMW
BMW Museum

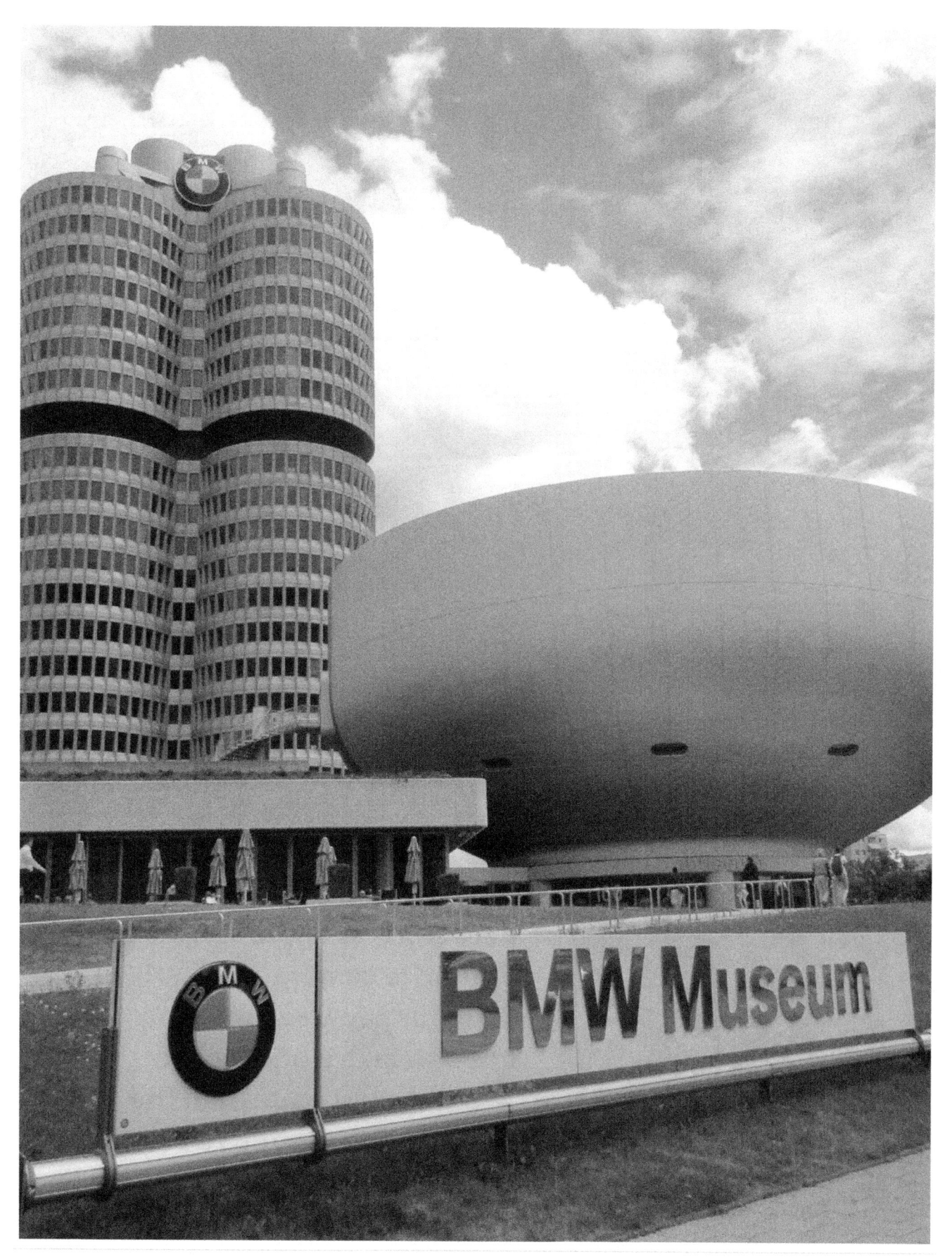

Frankfurt

SCAN HERE

HOW TO USE QR CODE

- Open your phone's camera app or download scanner app from play store or apple store
- Point the camera at the QR code for a few seconds (no need to take a photo).
- A link should appear on the display, leading you to the location of the code

Römerberg

🚶 69 hr
301 km

✈ 67 hr
291 km

Würzburg
Mannheim
Römerberg
Heilbronn

SCAN HERE

HOW TO USE QR CODE

- Open your phone's camera app or download scanner app from play store or apple store
- Point the camera at the QR code for a few seconds (no need to take a photo).
- A link should appear on the display, leading you to the location of the code

Hamburg

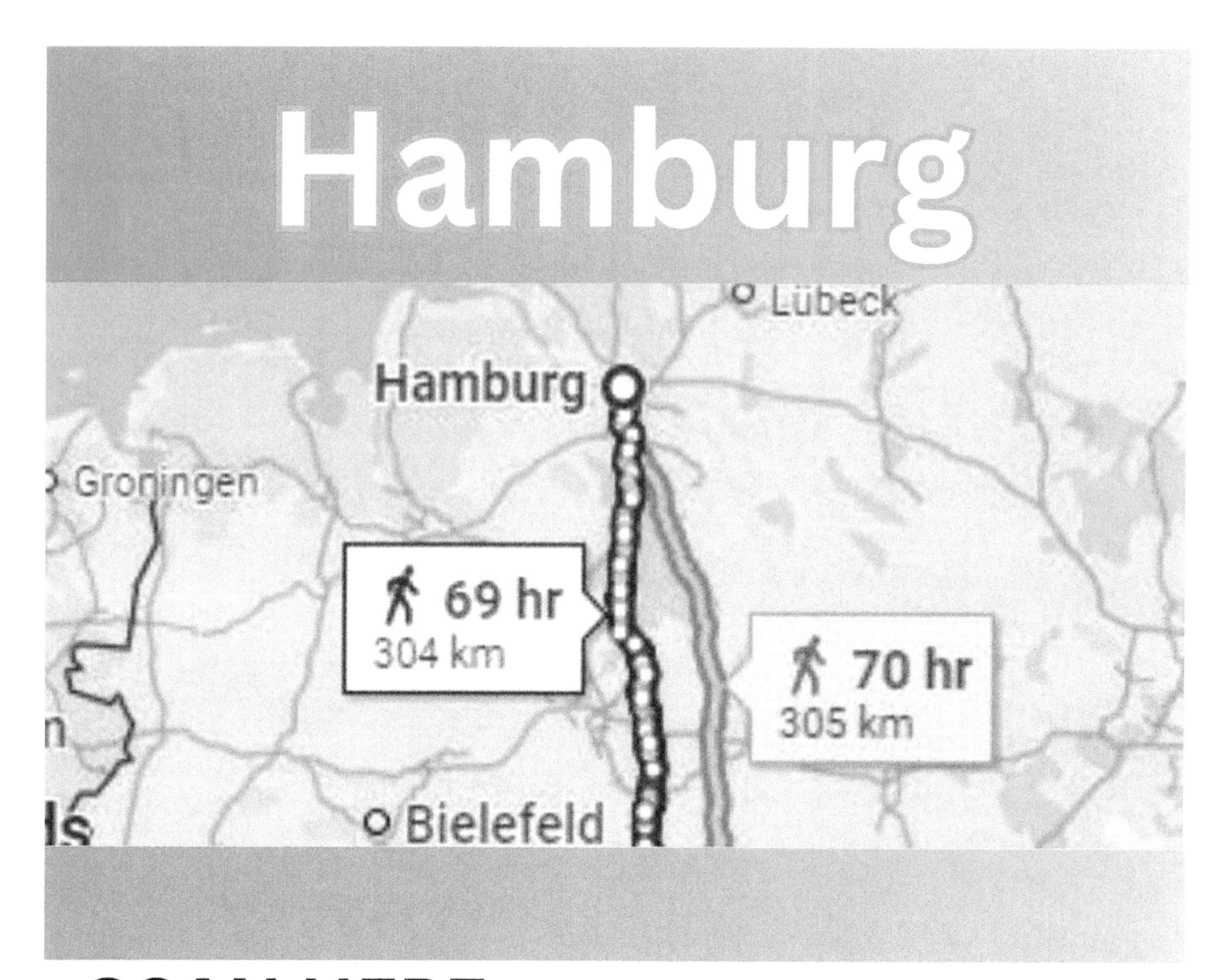

SCAN HERE

HOW TO USE QR CODE

- Open your phone's camera app or download scanner app from play store or apple store
- Point the camera at the QR code for a few seconds (no need to take a photo).
- A link should appear on the display, leading you to the location of the code

Cologne

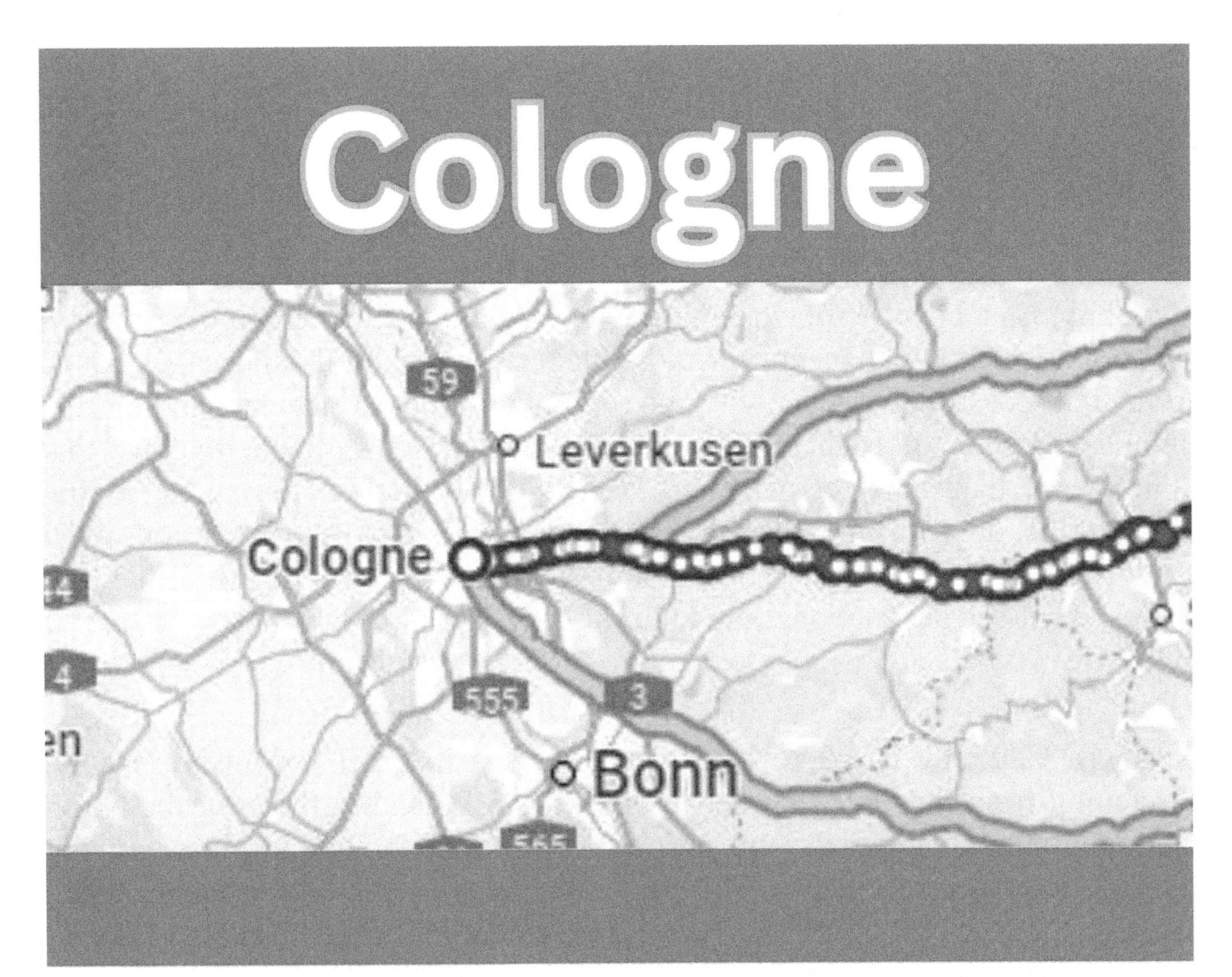

SCAN HERE

HOW TO USE QR CODE

- Open your phone's camera app or download scanner app from play store or apple store
- Point the camera at the QR code for a few seconds (no need to take a photo).
- A link should appear on the display, leading you to the location of the code

Chapter 4

Navigating Germany's Regions

Germany is a country of striking regional contrasts, where modern cities seamlessly blend with centuries-old villages, and natural landscapes range from flat coastlines to snow-capped mountain peaks. Understanding the unique character of each region enables travelers to craft an itinerary that aligns with their interests-whether exploring world-class museums, hiking alpine trails, or savoring wines along historic riverbanks. In this section, we'll explore Germany by region-north, south, east, and west-highlighting the best routes, must-see destinations, and cultural landmarks in each area.

Northern Germany

Northern Germany is where land meets the sea in quiet, expansive beauty. Stretching from the Dutch border in the west to Poland in the east, the North German Plain is flat, windswept and fertile, dotted with wind turbines, grazing livestock, and quaint villages. This region openness gives way to the powerful coastlines of the North Sea and Baltic Sea, where maritime heritage is deeply rooted in daily life and regional identity.

The climate is cooler and windier than in the south, with fresh sea breezes and dramatic skies adding to the unique charm of the landscape. You'll find dikes protecting low-lying lands, lighthouses perched at rugged edges, and fishing harbors where tradition lives on.

The Best Routes for Visiting Hamburg, Bremen, and Lübeck

1. Hamburg-Germany's Maritime Metropolis

Start your northern adventure in Hamburg, the second-largest city in Germany and arguably it's most international. Known for its colossal port, the third-largest in Europe, Hamburg offers a compelling mix of old and new. From the UNESCO-designated Speicherstadt (the world's largest warehouse complex) to the sleek Elbphilharmonie concert hall, the city pulses with cultural energy.

What to See: Elbphilharmonie Miniatur Wunderland, HafenCity, Reeperbahn nightlife district, Alster Lake.

Tip: Take a harbor boat tour for a unique view of the docks and skyline.

2. Bremen-Fairy Tales and Trading Power

A short drive southwest of Hamburg along the A1, Bremen is one of German most historic cities. It was a key player in the Hanseatic League and still retains a medieval heart, particularly around its Market Square.

Highlights: The Bremen Town Musicians statue, the Gothic Town Hall, the Roland Statue (both UNESCO World Heritage), and the Schnoor quarter.

3. Lübeck-The Queen of the Hanseatic League

Nestled along the northern coast of Germany, Lübeck stands as a testament to the rich maritime history and economic prowess of the Hanseatic League. Founded in the 12th century, this historic city quickly rose to prominence due to its strategic location along vital trade routes, becoming a vital hub for commerce, culture, and craftsmanship.

Must-See: St. Mary's Church, the Hospital of the Holy Spirit, marzipan shops at Niederegger, and the Hansemuseum.

Tip: Explore the old town on foot its compact and brimming with architectural treasures.

Coastal Attractions: North Sea and Baltic Sea Beaches

Germany might not be famous for beach holidays, but its northern coastline offers some stunning and surprising seaside experiences.

North Sea Coast-Tidal Flats and Island Escapes

The North Sea is defined by its Wadden Sea National Park, a UNESCO World Heritage Site known for its tidal mudflats. You can walk on the seabed during low tide (with a guide) from towns like Cuxhaven or Husum.

Baltic Sea Coast-Relaxed Resorts and Calm Waters

The Baltic coast has a gentler atmosphere. Think sandy beaches, pine forests, and elegant seaside architecture known as Bäderarchitektur.

Top Destinations: Timmendorfer Strand, Kühlungsborn, and Heiligendamm (Germany's oldest seaside resort).

Southern Germany

In complete contrast to the flat, breezy north, southern Germany rises into towering alpine peaks and rolling hills cloaked in forest. Here, you'll find Bavaria's postcard-perfect villages, half-timbered houses, onion-domed churches, and cows grazing in lush mountain meadows.

The Bavarian Alps

Stretching along Germany's southern border with Austria, the Bavarian Alps offer the most dramatic scenery in the country. This is where alpine traditions like lederhosen, yodeling, and hearty cuisine are very much alive.

Activities: Skiing, paragliding, mountain hiking, beer garden hopping.

Tip: Visit in late September for Alpine cattle drives (Almabtrieb) or during Christmas for snow-covered magic.

The Black Forest (Schwarzwald)

West of the Alps lies the Black Forest, a mystical land of dense woodlands, cuckoo clocks, and mineral spas.

Drive: Take the Schwarzwaldhochstraße (B500) a winding scenic route through the forest with lookout points and hiking trails.

Towns to Visit: Freiburg, Baden-Baden, and Triberg (home to Germany's highest waterfall and clock museum)..

Scenic Drives from Munich to Garmisch-Partenkirchen

One of Germany's most beautiful drives, the route from Munich to Garmisch-Partenkirchen covers approximately 90 kilometers of changing scenery, with suburban sprawl giving way to mountain vistas.

Attractions in Garmisch: Zugspitze (Germany's highest mountain), Partnach Gorge, and traditional alpine houses with painted facades.

This drive is spectacular in autumn (for colorful foliage), winter (for skiing), and spring (for alpine blooms).

Historical Sites

1. Neuschwanstein Castle-The Fantasy Brought to Life

Nestled in the hills near Füssen, Neuschwanstein Castle was commissioned by King Ludwig II of Bavaria and remains one of the most visited castles in Europe. With turrets piercing the clouds and mist rising from the valley, it's no surprise this was the inspiration for Disney's Cinderella Castle.

2. Zugspitze Mountain-Germany's Highest Point

Towering at 2,962 meters, Zugspitze offers panoramic views over the Alps and into neighboring Austria. The summit can be reached via a cogwheel train or the Eibsee cable car, both departing near Garmisch.

Eastern Germany

Following reunification in 1990, Eastern Germany underwent a remarkable transformation, evolving from decades of division into a vibrant and multifaceted region that blends historic charm with contemporary innovation. From Berlin vibrant cultural scene to Dresden's stunning baroque architecture and Leipzig's storied musical heritage, this part of Germany offers travelers authentic experiences, resilience, and a deep sense of historical roots.

Discovering Berlin's Vibrant Culture and History

Berlin is not just the capital of Germany; it is the symbolic heart of its past, present, and future. A city reborn from the ashes of war and division, Berlin today is a thrilling mix of gritty history, world-class museums, and alternative subcultures.

A City of Layers

Historic Berlin reveals stories of empire, war, and division. Start at the Brandenburg Gate, once isolated by the Berlin Wall, and walk down the Unter den Linden Boulevard to encounter history at every turn, Humboldt University, Museum Island, and the Berlin Cathedral.

Cold War Legacy: Visit Checkpoint Charlie, the Berlin Wall Memorial, and East Side Gallery—a preserved stretch of the wall turned into an open-air gallery with politically charged murals.

Museums and Art: The Pergamon Museum, Alte Nationalgalerie, and Jewish Museum are must-sees for history buffs and art lovers alike.

Modern Berlin

Neighborhood Life: Explore Berlin's distinct districts—from the artsy cafes and street art of Kreuzberg to the gentrified elegance of Prenzlauer Berg and the government institutions in Mitte.

Nightlife: Known globally for its electronic music scene, Berlin is home to legendary clubs like Berghain and Sisyphos.

Must-See Sights

1. Zwinger Palace: An ornate complex housing world-class museums like the Old Masters Picture Gallery.

2. Semper Opera House: One of Europe's most beautiful opera venues with a rich performance tradition.

Cultural Tip

Dresden is part of Saxony, a state with its proud traditions from Meissen porcelain to regional wines grown in the Elbe Valley.

Driving Route

Access Dresden via A4 or A17. Take a detour to the Saxon Switzerland National Park for breathtaking sandstone cliffs and hiking trails.

Leipzig: Modern Art Scene and Musical Heritage

Just 90 minutes from Berlin by car or train, Leipzig has emerged as one of Germany's most exciting cities, combining artistic innovation, musical roots, and an entrepreneurial spirit. It's where classical heritage and underground cool coexist.

Local Experience

Stroll through the Augustusplatz, stop by Auerbachs Keller (a historic pub mentioned in Goethe's Faust), or picnic at Clara-Zetkin Park.

Western Germany

Western Germany unfolds as a rich mosaic of lush wine country, historical cities, and industrious heritage. The Rhine River, one of Europe's most romantic waterways, flows through this region, flanked by medieval castles, terraced vineyards, and bustling towns that combine tradition and modernity.

The Rhine Valley and Wine Regions of Rhineland-Palatinate

The Upper Middle Rhine Valley, a UNESCO World Heritage Site, offers one of Europe's most beautiful river landscapes. From Koblenz to Bingen, the winding road hugs the river as it curves past castles, ruins, and charming wine villages.

Top Highlights

Lorelei Rock: The legendary cliff steeped in myth and river folklore.

Marksburg Castle and Burg Eltz: Among the few castles never destroyed, offering fully furnished rooms and medieval armories.

Wine Country

The Moselle Valley (a tributary of the Rhine) is a haven for Riesling lovers. Drive the Mosel Wine Route and stop at villages like Cochem, Bernkastell-Kues, and Traben-Trarbach.

Tips: Visit during harvest season (late September to early October) for wine festivals and tastings.

Exploring Cologne, Düsseldorf, and Bonn

These three cities, each situated along the Rhine, offer a trio of distinct experiences spanning ancient cathedrals, fashion capitals, and Beethoven's legacy.

Cologne (Köln): Gothic Grandeur and Carnival Energy

Cultural Highlights: Roman-Germanic Museum, Ludwig Museum for Modern Art.

Famous for: Kölsch beer served in small glasses and often accompanied by hearty fare.

Düsseldorf: Fashion, Art, and Business

As a global trade and fashion hub, Düsseldorf dazzles with Königsallee (one of Europe's most elegant shopping streets), avant-garde architecture in MedienHafen, and world-renowned art academies.

The Industrial Legacy of the Ruhr Area

At the heart of Germany's economic engine lies the Ruhrgebiet (Ruhr Region) a sprawling industrial belt that includes Essen, Dortmund, Duisburg, and Bochum. While historically known for coal and steel, the Ruhr has rebranded itself as a hub of culture, technology, and green transformation.

Key Attractions

1. Zeche Zollverein (Essen): A UNESCO-listed former coal mine turned cultural site, now housing museums, design centers, and performance spaces.

2. Gasometer Oberhausen: A towering industrial structure repurposed for immersive art installations.

Cultural Scene

The Ruhrtriennale Arts Festival and numerous theaters and galleries reflect a thriving creative scene that's uniquely urban and post-industrial.

From the windswept beaches of the north to the snow-covered peaks of the south, and from vibrant metropolises in the east to vineyard-laced river valleys in the west, Germany's regions each offer their charm and character. For travelers navigating by car, these regional distinctions create the perfect opportunity for customized adventures. Whether you're seeking history, nature, food, or culture, Germany's diverse landscapes and well-connected roadways make it an ideal country to explore at your own pace.

HafenCity

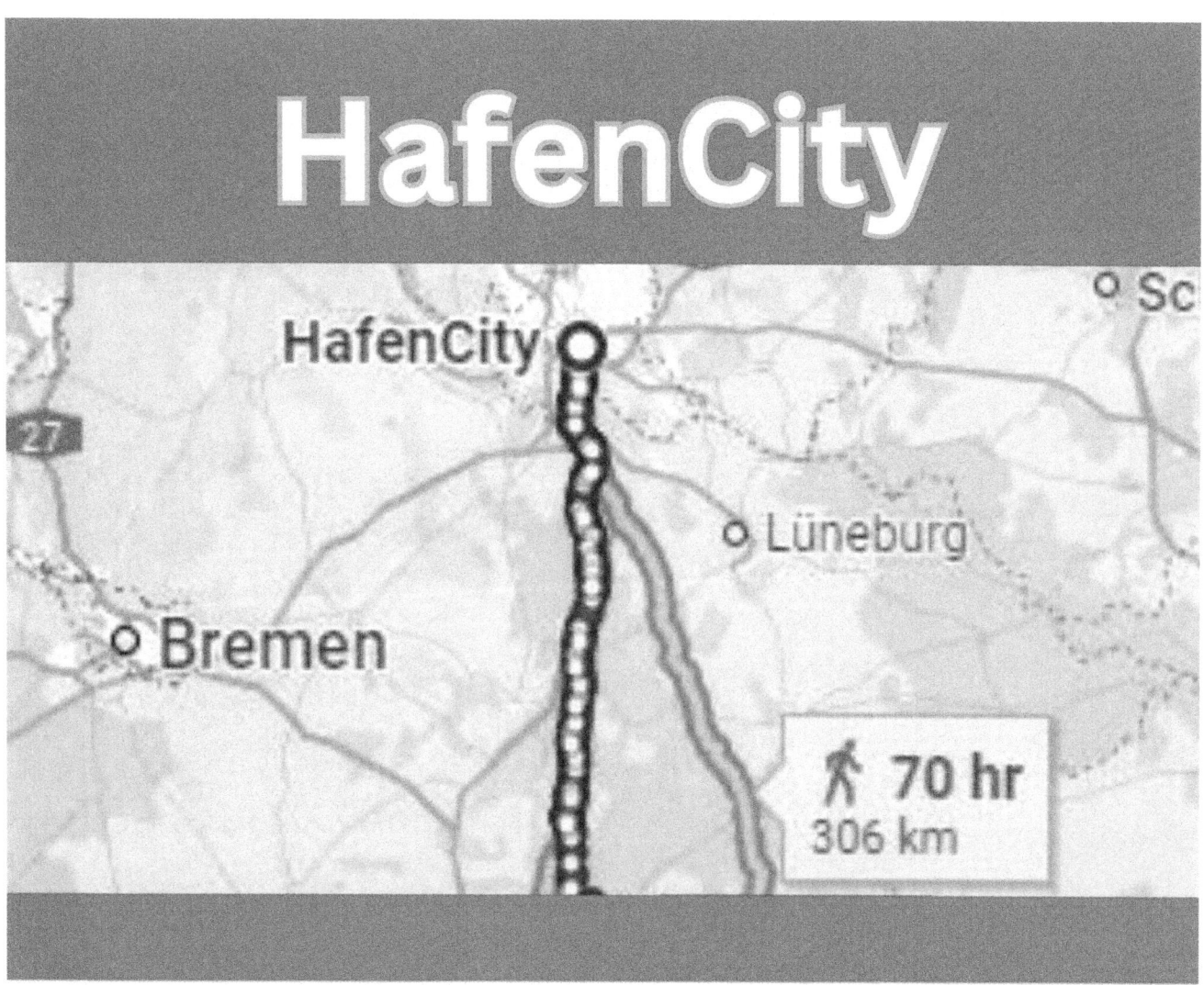

🚶 70 hr
306 km

SCAN HERE

HOW TO USE QR CODE

- Open your phone's camera app or download scanner app from play store or apple store
- Point the camera at the QR code for a few seconds (no need to take a photo).
- A link should appear on the display, leading you to the location of the code

Alster Lakes

Bremen

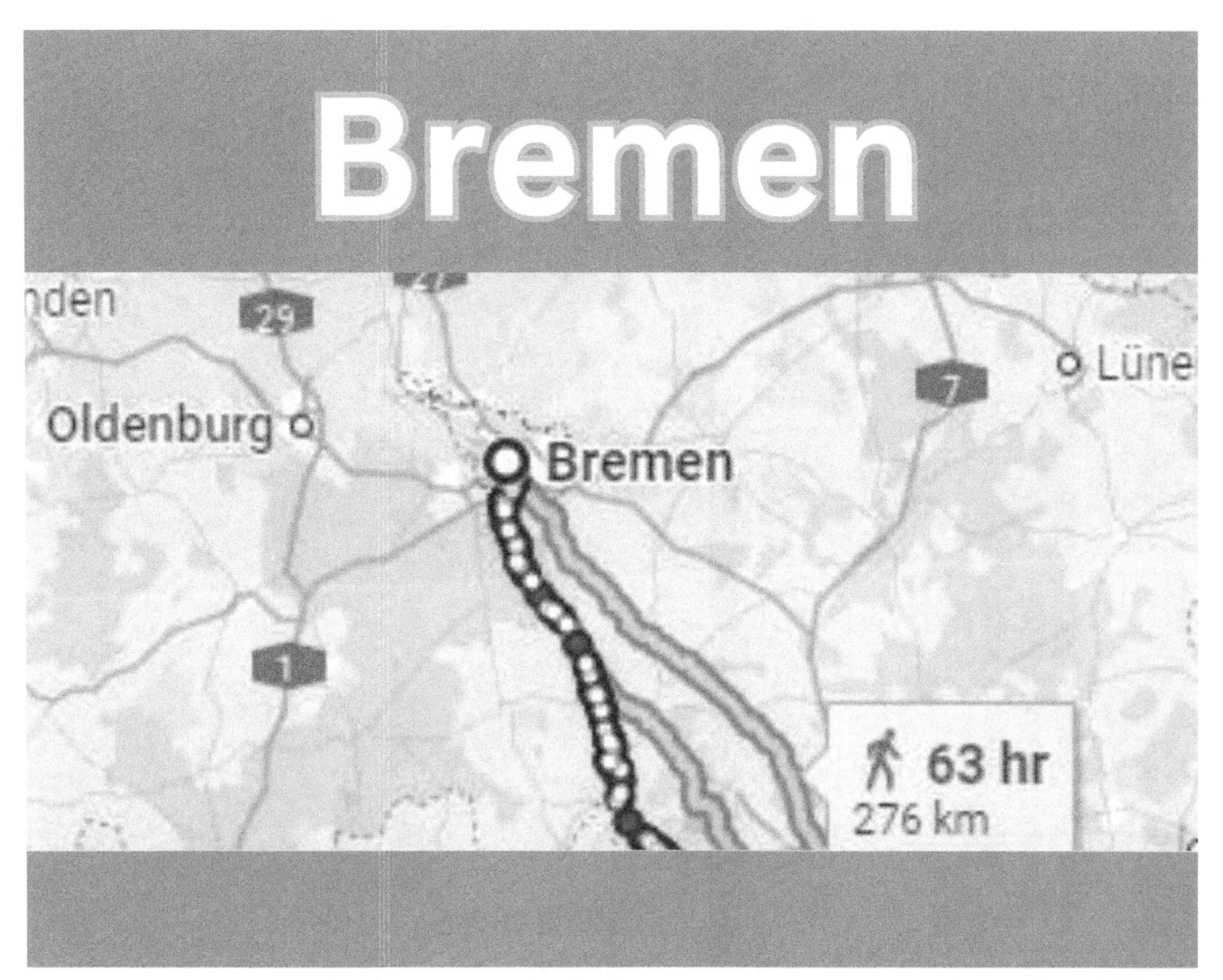

🚶 63 hr
276 km

SCAN HERE

HOW TO USE QR CODE

- Open your phone's camera app or download scanner app from play store or apple store
- Point the camera at the QR code for a few seconds (no need to take a photo).
- A link should appear on the display, leading you to the location of the code

Town Musicians of Bremen

St. Mary's Church

Hospital of the Holy Spirit

Wadden Sea National Park

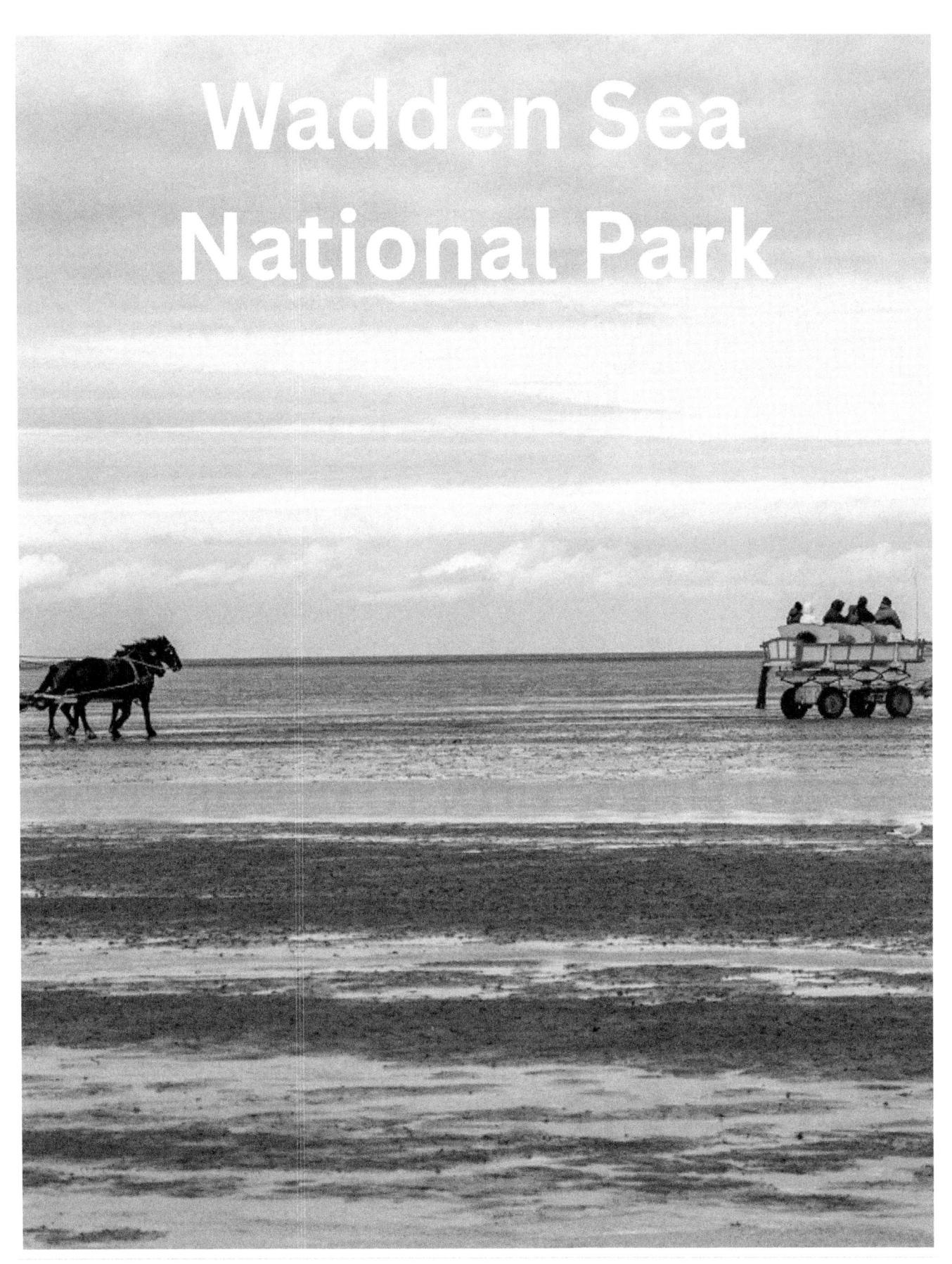

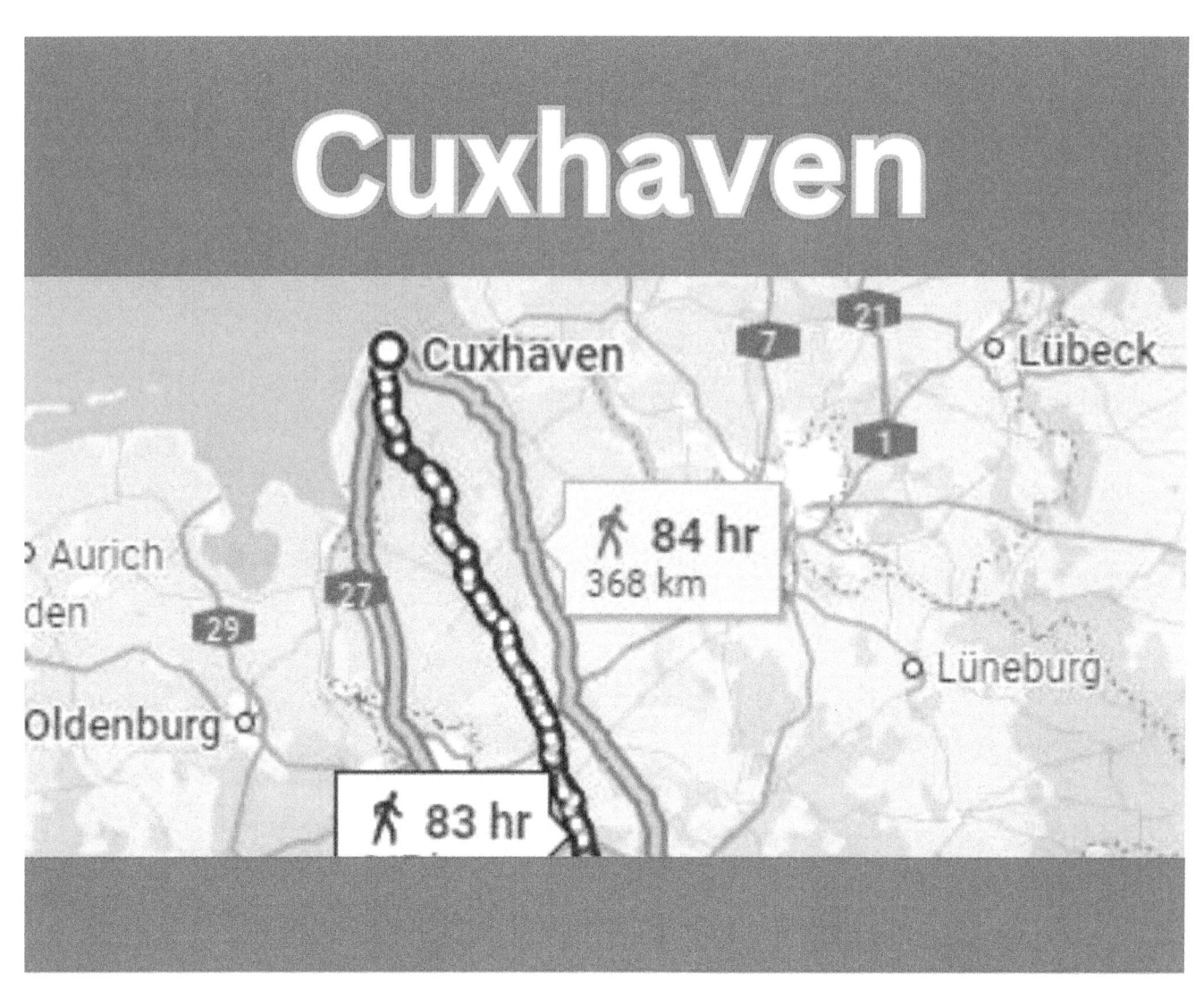

Cuxhaven

SCAN HERE

HOW TO USE QR CODE

- Open your phone's camera app or download scanner app from play store or apple store
- Point the camera at the QR code for a few seconds (no need to take a photo).
- A link should appear on the display, leading you to the location of the code

82 | Page

Timmendorfer Strand

Heiligendamm

Freiburg

SCAN HERE

HOW TO USE QR CODE

- Open your phone's camera app or download scanner app from play store or apple store
- Point the camera at the QR code for a few seconds (no need to take a photo).
- A link should appear on the display, leading you to the location of the code

Triberg

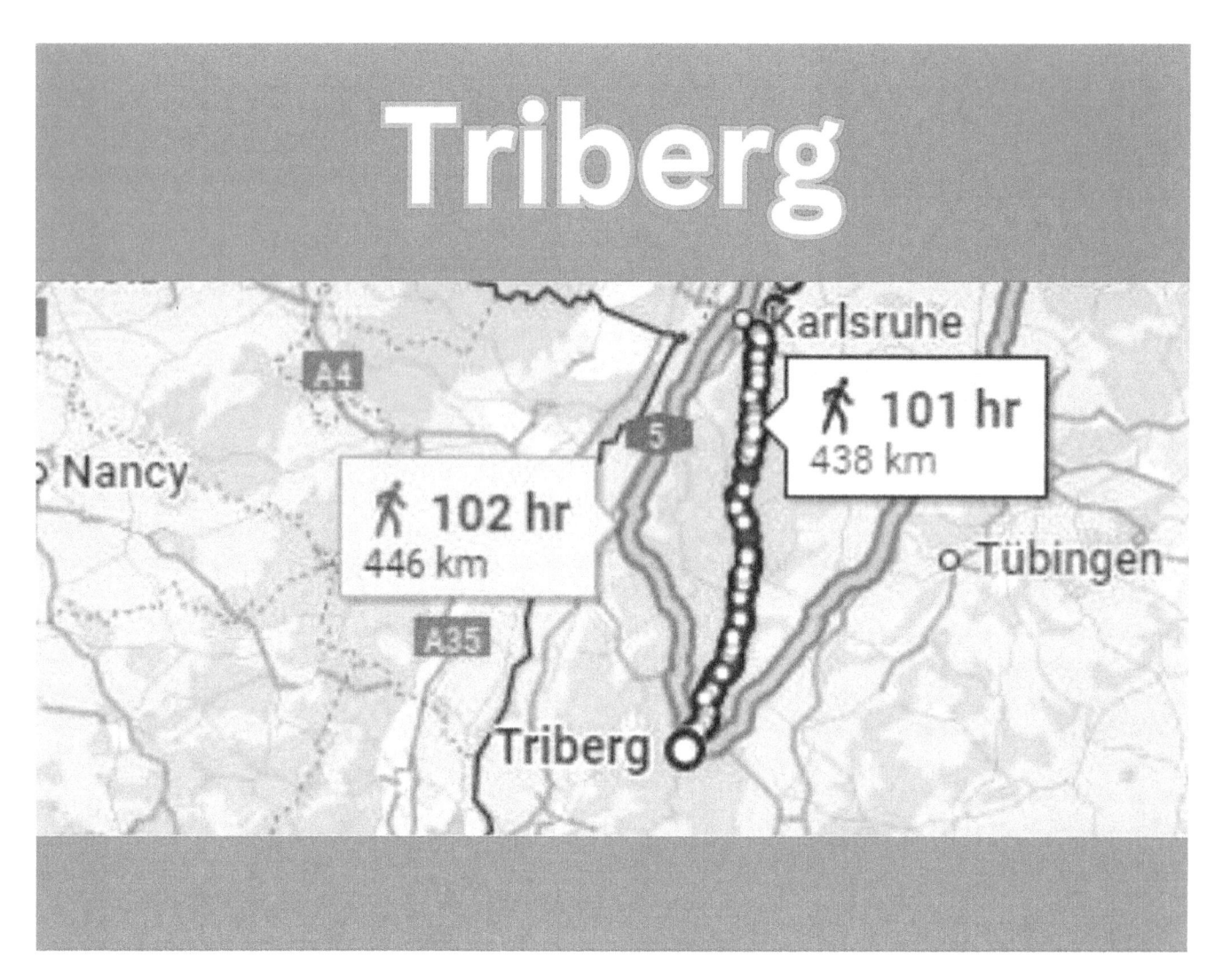

SCAN HERE

HOW TO USE QR CODE

- Open your phone's camera app or download scanner app from play store or apple store
- Point the camera at the QR code for a few seconds (no need to take a photo).
- A link should appear on the display, leading you to the location of the code

Zugspitze Mountain

Humboldt University of Berlin

Berlin Cathedral

Alte Nationalgalerie

Berghain Panorama Bar

Dresden Zwinger

Leipzig

🚶 34 hr
152 km

🚶 34 hr
152 km

SCAN HERE

HOW TO USE QR CODE

- Open your phone's camera app or download scanner app from play store or apple store
- Point the camera at the QR code for a few seconds (no need to take a photo).
- A link should appear on the display, leading you to the location of the code

Lorelei Rock

Marksburg

Cologne

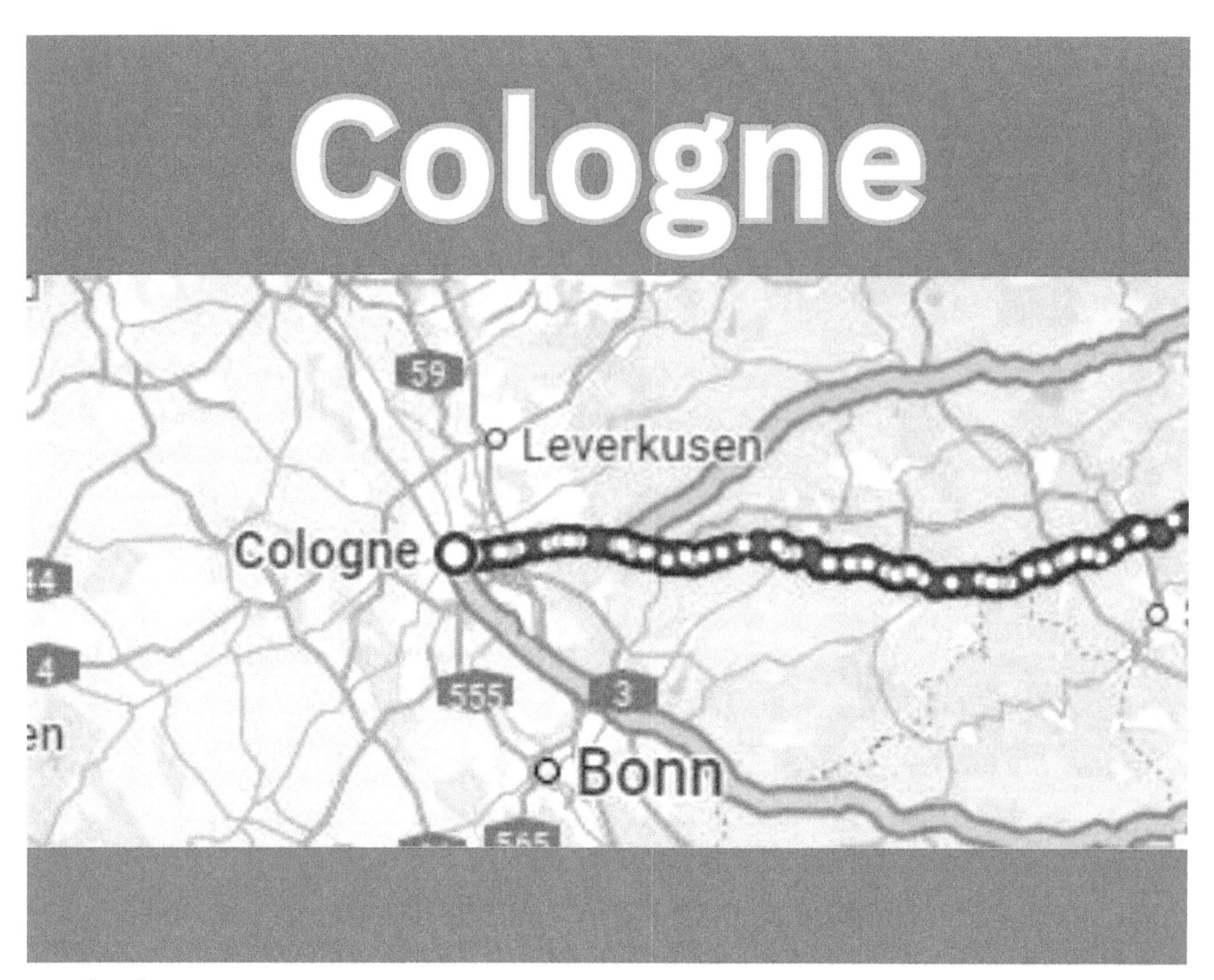

SCAN HERE

HOW TO USE QR CODE

- Open your phone's camera app or download scanner app from play store or apple store
- Point the camera at the QR code for a few seconds (no need to take a photo).
- A link should appear on the display, leading you to the location of the code

Düsseldorf

🚶 69 hr
299 km

SCAN HERE

HOW TO USE QR CODE

- Open your phone's camera app or download scanner app from play store or apple store
- Point the camera at the QR code for a few seconds (no need to take a photo).
- A link should appear on the display, leading you to the location of the code

Bonn

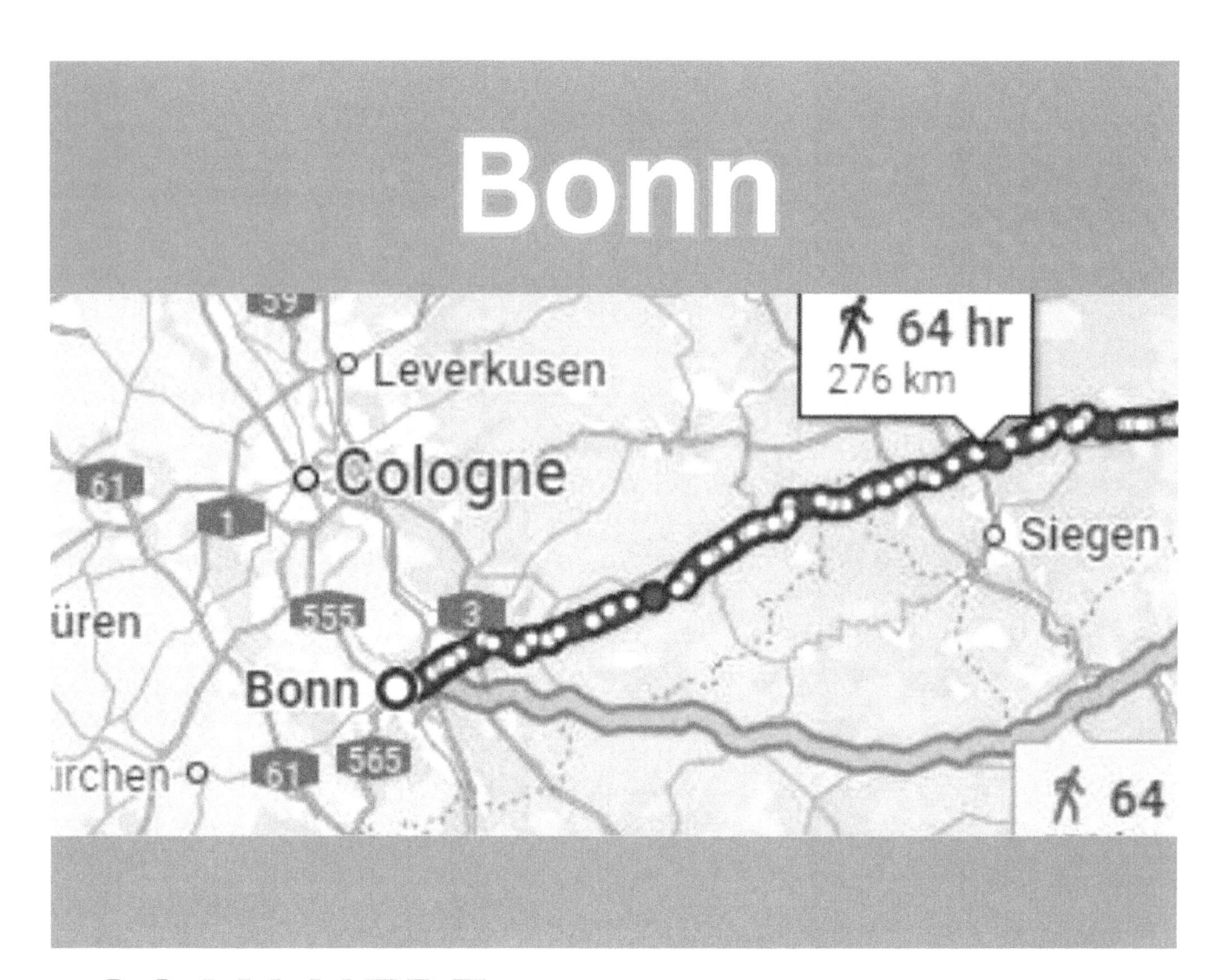

SCAN HERE

HOW TO USE QR CODE

- Open your phone's camera app or download scanner app from play store or apple store
- Point the camera at the QR code for a few seconds (no need to take a photo).
- A link should appear on the display, leading you to the location of the code

Dortmund

🚶 55 hr
241 km

SCAN HERE

HOW TO USE QR CODE

- Open your phone's camera app or download scanner app from play store or apple store
- Point the camera at the QR code for a few seconds (no need to take a photo).
- A link should appear on the display, leading you to the location of the code

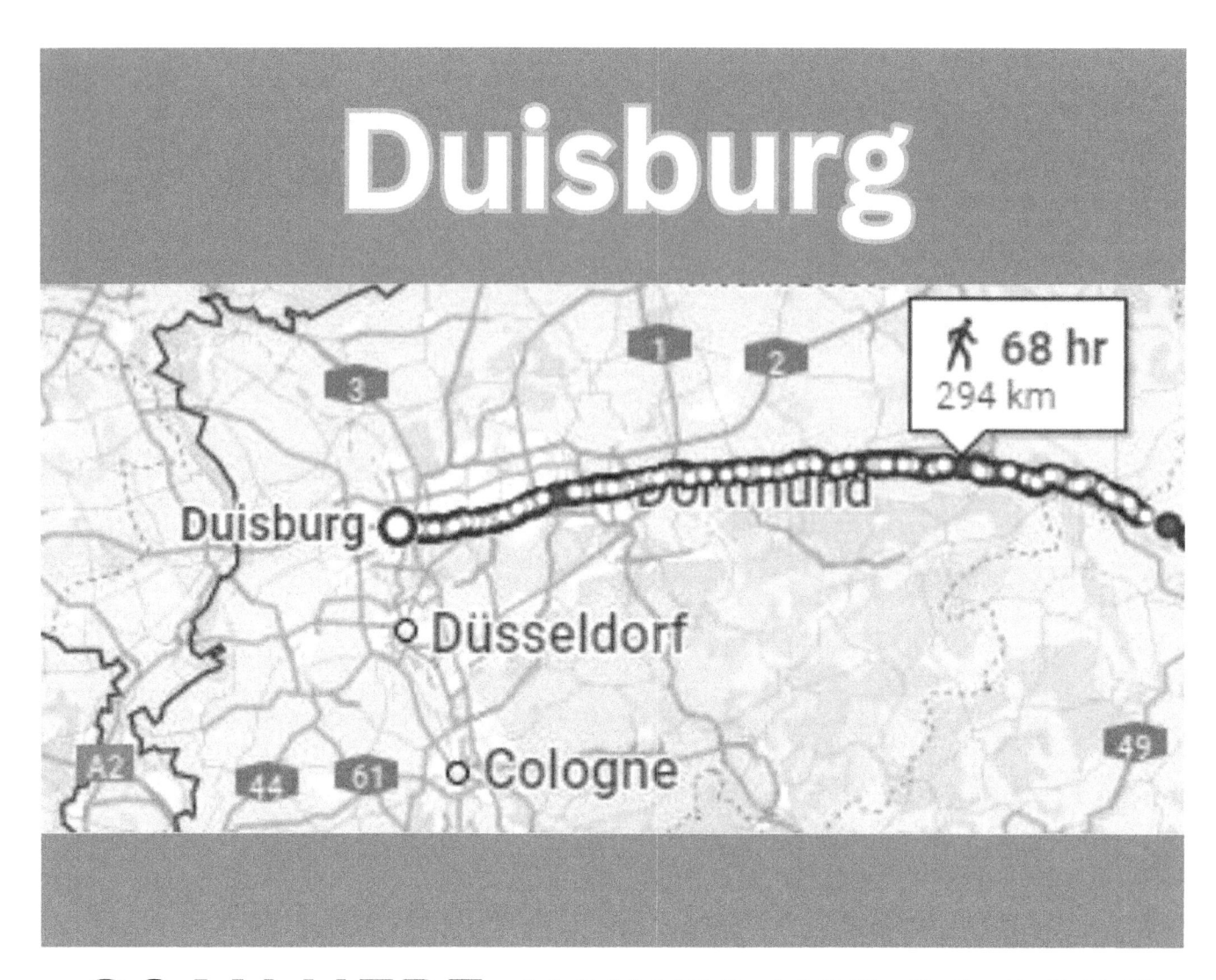

Duisburg

🚶 68 hr
294 km

SCAN HERE

HOW TO USE QR CODE

- Open your phone's camera app or download scanner app from play store or apple store
- Point the camera at the QR code for a few seconds (no need to take a photo).
- A link should appear on the display, leading you to the location of the code

Bochum

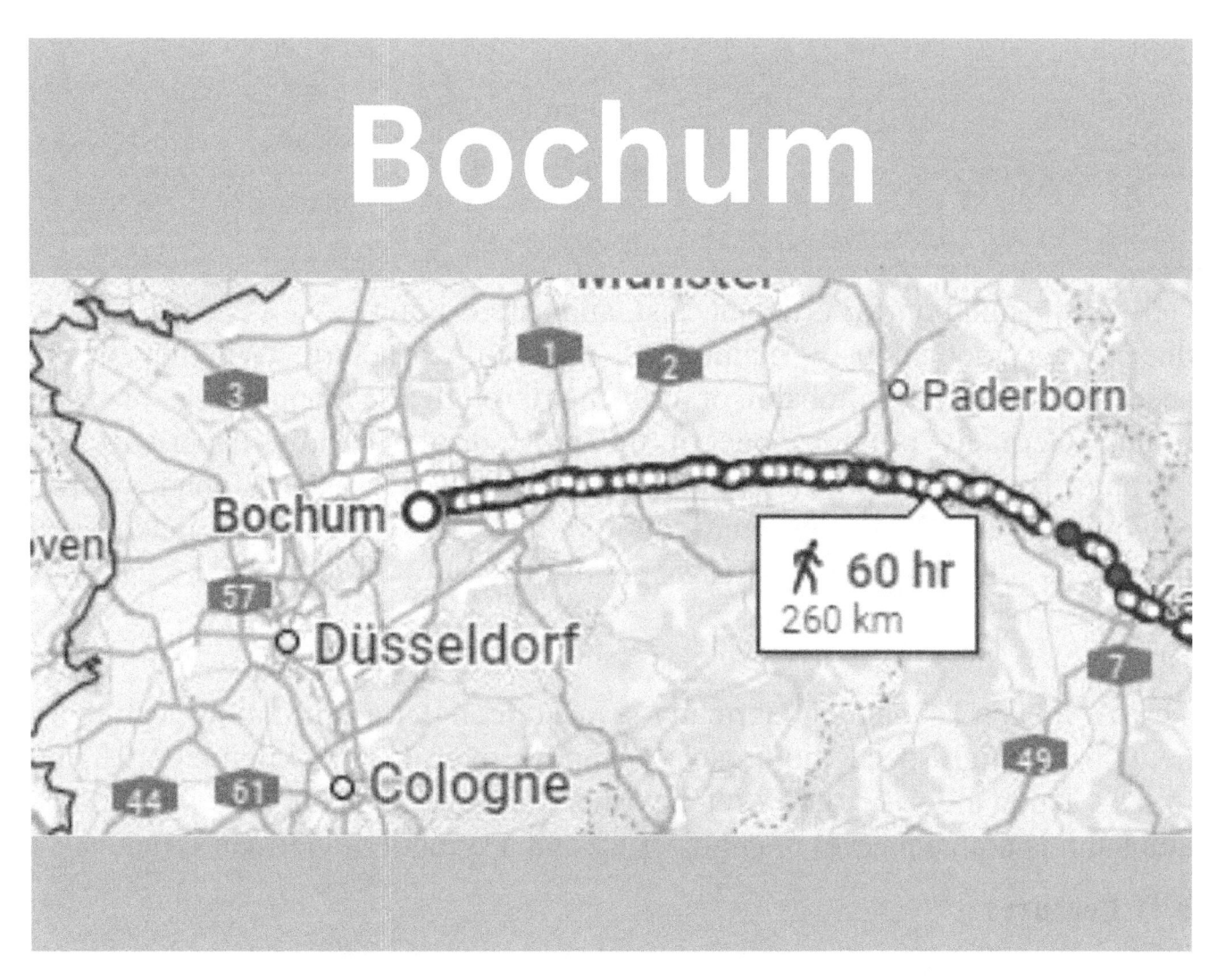

🚶 60 hr
260 km

SCAN HERE

HOW TO USE QR CODE

- Open your phone's camera app or download scanner app from play store or apple store
- Point the camera at the QR code for a few seconds (no need to take a photo).
- A link should appear on the display, leading you to the location of the code

Chapter 5

Major Highways and Road Networks

Germany reputation for efficient, fast, and safe driving is well-earned, largely due to its meticulously maintained road infrastructure. Whether you're speeding along the autobahn or cruising through the countryside on rural routes, Germany provides one of the most driver-friendly experiences in Europe. This section will explore the layout of Germany's road system, essential driving practices, and the top navigational tools to make your journey as smooth and stress-free as possible.

Autobahns Germany's World-Famous Highways

The Autobahn is one of Germany's most iconic transportation features a network of high-speed motorways spanning over 13,000 kilometers (8,000 miles). Known for certain stretches that have no general speed limit, the autobahn is both a marvel of engineering and a symbol of German efficiency.

Key Features

- Designated with an "A" followed by a number (e.g., A3, A9).
- Multiple lanes (usually 2–3 in each direction).
- Divided highways with emergency lanes and frequent rest areas.
- No tolls for private vehicles (except for specific tunnels and bridges).

Contrary to popular belief, not all parts of the autobahn are limitless. Many segments, especially near cities, construction zones, or areas with frequent congestion, have posted speed restrictions, often ranging from 100–130 km/h (62–81 mph).

Best Practices for Driving on the Autobahn

While exhilarating, driving on the autobahn requires attention, discipline, and an understanding of etiquette.

1. Keep Right Unless Overtaking

The left lane is strictly for overtaking. After passing, return promptly to the right lane. Staying in the left lane unnecessarily is not only discouraged, it's illegal.

2. No Passing on the Right

Overtaking on the right is prohibited. Always pass vehicles on the left, even in slower traffic.

3. Use Mirrors Constantly

Cars may approach rapidly in the left lane often luxury models traveling upwards of 200 km/h (124 mph). Check mirrors frequently before changing lanes.

4. Stay Aware of Speed Changes

Electronic or temporary signs may reduce the speed limit in response to traffic, weather, or construction. Ignoring these can lead to heavy fines.

5. Be Prepared for Status (Traffic Jams)

Autobahns can back up quickly. Keep an eye on navigation apps for traffic updates and use designated rest areas if needed.

How to Handle High-Speed Zones Safely

While unlimited speed zones can be thrilling, they come with risks. It's essential to know your vehicle, your limits, and the road ahead.

Safety Tips

Stick to the recommended speed limit of 130 km/h (81 mph), even where there's no official restriction.

Maintain a large following distance. Stopping distances are much longer at high speeds.

Avoid sudden maneuvers. Lane changes should be smooth and well-signaled.

Check tire pressure and vehicle condition before long-distance drives.

Stay alert high-speed driving requires maximum focus.

Motorways and Federal Roads

While the autobahn often gets the spotlight, Germany also boasts a robust system of Bundesstraßen (federal roads) and Landstraßen (state or rural roads).

The Network of Bundesstraßen

Marked with a "B" followed by a number (e.g., B1, B9), Bundesstraßen are vital connectors between towns, cities, and regions. These are well-maintained highways, usually with one lane in each direction, and may pass through towns or scenic rural areas.

Why They Matter

Serve as feeder roads to the autobahns.

Offer more scenic and cultural experiences than high-speed routes.

Ideal for slower-paced travel, especially for those avoiding tolls or in RVs.

Driving Tips for Rural Roads and Country Lanes

Germany's countryside is dotted with winding roads, forest tracks, and village streets that provide a more intimate view of the country, but they come with their own driving challenges.

What to Expect

Narrow roads, especially in the Black Forest or Alpine areas.

Tractors, cyclists, and wildlife on roads drive cautiously.

Speed limits are typically capped at 100 km/h (62 mph), but are often lower in small towns or hilly terrain.

Tips for Safe Rural Driving:

Be ready for sudden stops, blind curves, and steep inclines are common.

Use headlights in shaded areas or tunnels.

Watch for signs indicating priority at unmarked intersections.

Fuel stations may be sparse fill up when you can.

Drive responsibly to protect the natural landscape and respect local residents.

Reduce speed in areas with high wildlife activity and always stay vigilant.

Approach intersections slowly, and watch for vehicles or pedestrians entering or exiting.

Navigational Tools

Planning and navigating your trip through Germany is easier than ever, thanks to a range of modern and traditional tools. Whether you're using cutting-edge tech or keeping a paper backup, preparation is key.

Top GPS Apps and Tools

1. Google Maps: Offers turn-by-turn navigation, real-time traffic data, and offline map downloads.

2. Waze: Crowdsourced traffic updates, including police alerts, road closures, and accident warnings.

3. HERE WeGo: Strong offline navigation features and excellent public transport integration.

4. Language and Translation Tools: Language barriers can sometimes pose challenges. Language translation apps like Google Translate can assist in understanding signage, asking for directions, or communicating with locals.

Tips for Effective Navigation

- Always keep an updated digital and physical map handy.
- Confirm routes and transportation schedules in advance.
- Be aware of local traffic laws and road signs.
- Carry a power bank to keep your devices charged.
- Stay informed about weather conditions that may affect travel plans.

Offline Maps and Paper Maps for Backup

While GPS apps are reliable, it's smart to have a backup navigation system, especially when driving through mountainous or remote areas.

Offline Options

Google Maps Offline: Download maps before your trip.

Maps.me: Detailed maps that work entirely offline.

Michelin Guide Maps: Known for detailed scenic routes and local tips.

Paper Maps

ADAC (Germany's automobile club) publishes excellent road maps.

Buy maps from local tourist offices, fuel stations, or bookstores.

Mark out scenic routes or rural detours for more flexibility.

Digital Route Planning with Real-Time Traffic Updates

In today's fast-paced world, efficient travel within Germany relies heavily on advanced digital tools that provide real-time traffic information. Modern route planning applications have transformed the way travelers navigate, offering dynamic guidance that adapts to current road conditions, accidents, and congestion.

Benefits of Real-Time Traffic Updates

Time Efficiency: Adjust your journey based on real-time conditions, reducing travel time.

Recommended Tools

Google Maps Traffic Layer: Color-coded routes show traffic intensity.

TomTom GO App: Paid app with precise traffic and speed camera alerts.

Komoot: Ideal for planning bike or hiking detours along your drive.

Germany's road network is vast, varied, and exceptionally maintained. From the thrill of the autobahn to the serenity of rural back roads, the country offers driving experiences for every preference. By understanding the rules, preparing for conditions, and using the right tools, travelers can explore Germany with confidence and freedom. Whether you're planning a short regional tour or a cross-country expedition, navigating Germany's highways and byways will be a major highlight of your journey.

Bode Museum

Chapter 6

Regional Driving Laws and Special Considerations

Germany has established low-emission zones (Umweltzonen) in numerous major cities to combat air pollution and enhance urban air quality. These zones restrict access to vehicles that do not comply with certain environmental standards, especially regarding vehicle emissions.

Environmental Zones (Low Emission Zones)

Understanding "Umweltzone" and Emission Sticker Requirements

An "Umweltzone" (environmental zone) is an area within a city where access is restricted to vehicles based on their emissions. These zones are in place to protect both the environment and public health by reducing harmful pollutants such as nitrogen oxides (NOx) and particulate matter (PM).

Vehicles entering these zones are required to display an emission sticker (Umweltplakette), which indicates the vehicle's emission level. The stickers are color-coded according to Euro emission standards: green for the cleanest vehicles compliant with Euro 4, yellow for Euro 5, and red for Euro 6, representing the highest emissions among the categories.

To comply with these regulations

1. Green sticker: Vehicles that comply with Euro 4 or higher emission standards, including most new cars.

2. Yellow sticker: For vehicles meeting Euro 3 emissions standards, mostly older cars.

3. Red sticker: For vehicles that do not meet the Euro 3 standard, which are generally restricted from entering the most stringent zones.

Before entering cities such as Berlin, Frankfurt, and Munich, it's important to ensure your vehicle complies with the local environmental zone regulations. Visitors renting cars should also verify whether their vehicle is equipped with an appropriate sticker. In many cases, rental agencies can provide the necessary sticker if the vehicle is eligible.

The Importance of Having an Environmental Badge for Certain Cities

Cities with stringent environmental policies depend on these stickers to regulate vehicle access to specific areas. Failure to display the appropriate sticker can result in fines, and in certain cases, your vehicle may be denied entry at checkpoints. Beyond being a legal obligation, these stickers are essential for reducing environmental impact during your visit to Germany. Keep in mind that emission zone boundaries may vary according to local regulations, so it's important to check the current rules before driving.

Winter Driving

Driving during the winter months in Germany presents both unique challenges and rewarding experiences. The country's diverse terrain from the snowy peaks of the Alps to the chilly northern coast requires drivers to be well-prepared and attentive to changing conditions.

Mandatory Winter Tires and Safety Tips for Driving in Snow and Ice

In Germany, winter tires are mandatory from October to Easter (known as the "O" to "O" rule). This means that during the winter months, vehicles must be fitted with tires that are specifically designed to perform well in cold, icy, or snowy conditions. Winter tires feature deeper treads and are made of rubber compounds that remain flexible at low temperatures, improving traction on slippery surfaces.

When driving in snow or icy conditions, some key safety tips to keep in mind include:

1. Use Gentle Movements: Accelerate, brake, and steer smoothly to prevent losing control. Sudden movements can cause skidding on slippery surfaces.

2. Reduce your speed: Snow and ice make stopping distances much longer, so it's important to drive more cautiously and avoid sudden acceleration or braking.

3. Increase following distance: The roads will be slippery, so maintaining extra space between your vehicle and the one in front is crucial for avoiding accidents.

4. Use your headlights: During snowy or foggy conditions, make sure your headlights are on, even during the day, to increase your visibility and to ensure other drivers can see you clearly.

5. Keep a safe distance from snowplows: If you are driving on roads that have been recently cleared, stay behind snowplows to ensure safety and avoid being sprayed by the snow-clearing operations.

Best Practices for Dealing with Fog, Rain, and Slippery Roads

In addition to winter weather, Germany also experiences dense fog and heavy rainfall, which can make driving more hazardous.

Here are some key tips for dealing with fog, rain, and slippery roads:

1. Fog: In foggy conditions, it's crucial to reduce your speed and activate your fog lights if visibility becomes severely limited. Keep in mind that fog lights are designed specifically for foggy weather and should not be used during regular rain or snow.
2. Rain: Heavy rainfall can lead to slippery road conditions, especially on bridges and overpasses where water tends to accumulate quickly. Exercise caution to prevent hydroplaning, a situation in which your tires lose contact with the road surface. If you start to hydroplane, gently lift your foot off the accelerator and steer straight ahead until you regain control.
3. Slippery Roads: If roads are slippery due to rain, snow, or ice, avoid sharp turns and rapid speed changes. Drive smoothly to maintain grip on the road. The Anti-lock Braking System (ABS) can help during slippery conditions by preventing the wheels from locking when you brake.

Roundabouts and Traffic Circles

Roundabouts are a common feature of Germany's road infrastructure, particularly in cities and smaller towns. Knowing how to navigate these circular intersections will make your driving experience safer and more efficient.

How to Navigate Roundabouts in Germany

The basic rule in roundabouts is "give way to traffic from the left"—this means that vehicles already in the roundabout have the right of way. Before entering a roundabout, be sure to yield to any vehicles already in the circle, even if it means waiting for several minutes at times, especially in busy cities.

There are a few key guidelines to follow when navigating roundabouts:

1. Approaching the roundabout: Slow down and be prepared to stop if necessary. Indicate your intention to turn (either left or right) before entering.

2. Entering the roundabout: Look left before entering, and enter when there is a safe gap in traffic. If there are multiple lanes in the roundabout, use the appropriate lane for your exit.

3. Exiting the roundabout: Signal right before you exit the roundabout. Be aware that the exit lanes may be shared with other traffic, so always keep an eye out for pedestrians or cyclists.

Common Mistakes to Avoid When Entering or Exiting Roundabouts

1. Not yielding to traffic: This can cause confusion and accidents, especially in busy roundabouts.

2. Incorrect signaling: Always signal your intention to exit or change lanes, as this helps other drivers anticipate your movements.

3. Entering the wrong lane: Choose the right lane based on your planned exit to avoid having to cross other lanes inside the roundabout.

4. Exceeding the Speed Limit: Entering a roundabout at high speed reduces reaction time and can cause loss of control.

5. Not Using Turn Signal When Exiting: Many drivers forget to signal when leaving the roundabout, which can confuse other road users.

6. Ignoring Signage and Road Markings: Ignoring these cues can lead to wrong turns or dangerous maneuvers.

Pedestrian Zones

Germany is renowned for its vibrant city centers and historic districts, many of which feature dedicated pedestrian zones that prioritize foot traffic and enhance urban livability. These areas are thoughtfully designed to promote sustainable mobility, support local businesses, and provide residents and visitors with safe and enjoyable environments for shopping, leisure, and cultural experiences.

Understanding Pedestrian-Only Areas in City Centers

Pedestrian zones (Fußgängerzonen) are marked with signs that indicate that only pedestrians are allowed. However, some zones may permit delivery vehicles during certain hours or allow access for residents or authorized vehicles. It's important to familiarize yourself with the specific rules for each area.

Key Features of Pedestrian Zones

Restricted Vehicle Access: Most pedestrian zones limit or completely ban vehicle entry, allowing only authorized vehicles such as delivery trucks during certain hours or residents with special permits. This creates a safer and more inviting space for pedestrians.

Enhanced Urban Atmosphere: Streets are often lined with cafes, shops, and cultural landmarks, fostering a lively atmosphere. Wide walkways, street furniture, landscaping, and public art contribute to the aesthetic appeal.

What to Do If You Need to Park Near or in Pedestrian Zones

If you need to park near or within a pedestrian zone, check the local parking regulations. In some cases, there may be parking areas located on the outskirts of the pedestrian zone or in nearby garages. Be sure to follow any signs indicating whether or not parking is allowed. Also, be cautious about parking too close to these zones, as fines can be imposed for unauthorized parking.

While navigating these pedestrian areas, always remember to respect the local rules and prioritize the safety of pedestrians. Avoid driving or parking in pedestrian zones unless explicitly permitted, and ensure that you leave adequate space for people walking, especially in crowded areas.

Dolomiti Bellunesi National Park

Chapter 7

Accommodations and Places to Stay

Germany is known for offering a wide variety of accommodations to suit every traveler's needs. Whether you are embarking on a luxurious getaway, taking a budget-friendly road trip, or seeking an authentic cultural experience, Germany has something for everyone. In this section, we will explore the best accommodations available in Germany, from high-end hotels to cozy guesthouses, and dive into the options for those who prefer to travel with their own camping gear or camper van.

Hotel Options

Germany is home to a diverse range of hotels, from internationally renowned chains offering five-star luxury experiences to charming boutique hotels tucked in the heart of picturesque towns. No matter your budget or preference, the country provides a wide range of options.

From Luxury Hotels to Budget-Friendly Stays

For those seeking indulgence, Germany features several luxury hotel chains renowned for their world-class amenities and services. Popular brands such as Bulgari, Ritz-Carlton, and InterContinental have properties in major cities like Berlin, Munich, and Frankfurt. These upscale hotels offer opulent rooms, rooftop bars, fine dining establishments, and exclusive spas. Many luxury hotels also provide comprehensive concierge services to ensure guests enjoy the best of Germany, whether by arranging private tours or securing tickets to cultural events.

If you're looking to save money, Germany offers numerous affordable and budget-friendly hotel options. Well-known chains like Ibis, Motel One, and B&B Hotels provide modern, budget-conscious rooms often situated in convenient city-center locations. While these hotels may not feature luxury amenities, they deliver great value with clean accommodations, comfortable beds, and easy access to local attractions.

Best Hotel Chains and Boutique Hotels in Germany

Germany is also home to several boutique hotels that offer a more personal, unique, and often more intimate experience. Many boutique hotels are located in historic buildings or architecturally significant properties, allowing guests to experience the charm of traditional German architecture alongside modern amenities. These types of hotels are ideal for travelers who enjoy staying in places that reflect the local culture and ambiance.

Notable boutique hotel chains include 25hours Hotels, which have a unique, quirky style that appeals to younger travelers and design enthusiasts. Their properties in cities like Berlin, Hamburg, and Frankfurt are known for their vibrant interiors, thematic decor, and laid-back vibe. Another excellent option is Hotel Adlon Kempinski in Berlin, known for its luxurious setting and rich history, as it was once frequented by royalty and celebrities.

Booking Tips and Accommodations for Road Trip Travelers

If you're embarking on a road trip across Germany, it's important to consider your accommodation options carefully. While larger cities often offer a range of hotels, smaller towns and rural areas may have fewer options, so booking ahead is advised. Online booking platforms such as Booking.com, Airbnb, and Expedia allow travelers to book in advance, ensuring they have a place to stay along the way.

For road trip enthusiasts seeking flexibility, consider booking a mix of hotels, guesthouses, and Landgasthöfe (country inns). These establishments provide an authentic experience in more rural areas and often serve as centers of local culture and cuisine.

For spontaneous travelers, Germany's "Landgasthof" system allows you to stop and ask for availability along the way, perfect for those who enjoy the freedom of not being tied to a strict schedule. However, always double-check availability, particularly during peak seasons like summer or the Christmas holidays.

Camping and Caravanning

Germany is a country that embraces the outdoors, with thousands of campsites, RV parks, and scenic locations for camping and caravanning. Whether you're looking to park your RV near a lakeside or set up a tent in a forest, Germany offers countless opportunities for camping enthusiasts.

Best Campsites and RV Parks Across Germany

Germany's campsites (Campingplätze) and RV parks (Wohnmobilstellplätze) are well-maintained and often located in beautiful areas, such as near national parks, lakes, or historical towns. One popular region for camping is the Black Forest, where visitors can enjoy picturesque views, hiking trails, and cycling routes. The Rhine Valley is another top camping destination, offering both luxury and rustic campsites along the famous river.

The Bavarian Alps are perfect for those seeking adventure. Campgrounds in the region offer views of snow-capped mountains and some even provide opportunities for winter sports. If you're traveling with your camper van, Germany is home to many "stellplätze" designated areas where RVs can park overnight, often with amenities such as electricity, water, and waste disposal.

Camper Van Rentals and Essentials for Camping in Germany

For road trip enthusiasts who prefer the flexibility and comfort of a camper van, numerous companies offer rentals across the country. Popular rental agencies like McRent and CamperDays provide a range of camper vans, motorhomes, and caravans equipped with everything you need for a road trip. These vehicles typically come with kitchen facilities, a sleeping area, and an onboard bathroom, making them ideal for longer journeys.

When renting a camper van, it's important to pack accordingly, as storage space will be limited. Be sure to bring essentials such as sleeping bags, hiking boots, and warm clothing, particularly if you're traveling in the colder months. Also, familiarize yourself with local camping laws in Germany, especially regarding noise restrictions, waste disposal, and fire safety. Many campsites have clear guidelines to ensure that the natural beauty of Germany landscapes is preserved.

Hostels and Guesthouses

For budget-conscious travelers, youth hostels, local guesthouses, and bed-and-breakfasts (B&Bs) offer excellent alternatives to traditional hotels. Germany's hostel system is extensive, particularly in larger cities and popular tourist areas, and offers an affordable way to meet other travelers and explore the country without breaking the bank.

Youth Hostels, Local Guesthouses, and B&Bs

Vibrant cities and scenic towns await explorers across Germany. For travelers seeking a social atmosphere and opportunities to connect with others, hostels are a great choice. Notable options include The Circus Hostel in Berlin, a trendy and modern establishment offering a variety of private and shared rooms, and Meininger Hostel in Munich, recognized for its clean, functional accommodations and prime location.

For those seeking a more authentic experience, consider staying in local guesthouses (Pensions) or bed-and-breakfasts (B&Bs). These family-run establishments offer a warm, welcoming atmosphere and often serve delicious homemade breakfasts. Guesthouses can be found in both urban and rural areas, making them an excellent choice for anyone looking to immerse themselves in the local culture and community.

Popular Hostels in Major Cities and Scenic Regions

Some of the most popular hostels in major German cities include:

1. Wombats City Hostel (Berlin, Munich and Vienna): Known for its clean facilities and friendly atmosphere.

2. A&O Hostel (Multiple locations): A reliable budget option with locations across Germany, including Berlin, Hamburg, and Cologne.

3. EastSeven Berlin Hostel: A cozy, centrally located hostel in Berlin known for its vibrant communal spaces.

For travelers looking to explore Germany's beautiful countryside, the Black Forest, Bavarian Alps, and Lake Constance regions all have excellent guesthouses and B&Bs offering beautiful views and peaceful settings.

Local Cuisine and Food Stops

Germany is known for its hearty, flavorful cuisine, with each region offering unique specialties. From savory dishes like bratwurst and schnitzel to delicious pastries like pretzels, German food is rich in tradition and taste.

Must-Try German Foods

Some classic German dishes that you should definitely try include:

1. Bratwurst: A flavorful German sausage, typically made from pork, beef, or veal, and often served with mustard, sauerkraut, and potatoes.

2. Pretzels (Brezn): Soft, doughy, and sprinkled with coarse salt, pretzels are a quintessential German snack, often enjoyed with a cold beer.

3. Schnitzel: A breaded and deep-fried cutlet, typically made from pork or veal. The most famous version is Wiener schnitzel, which hails from Vienna but is popular throughout Germany.

4. Kartoffelsalat (Potato Salad): Often served as a side dish, potato salad can be made in many regional variations, including with mayonnaise or a warm vinegar-based dressing.

5. Sauerkraut: Fermented cabbage that's often paired with meats, especially sausages and pork dishes.

Regional Specialties from Bavaria, Swabia, and the Rhineland

1. Bavaria: Famous for Weißwurst (white sausages), pretzels, and hearty dishes like Schweinshaxe (roast pork knuckle).

2. Swabia: Known for Maultaschen (stuffed pasta) and Spätzle (egg noodles), which are often served with cheese and onions.

3. Rhineland: Famous for Himmel un Ääd (blood sausage with apples and mashed potatoes) and Rheinischer Sauerbraten (marinated beef pot roast).

Street Food and Local Snacks for a Quick Bite on the Go

Germany street food scene is vibrant and full of delicious options. Curry Rico (grilled sausage with curry ketchup) is a popular snack in many cities. Back

Kebab, a Turkish-German fusion dish, is also widely enjoyed. For a lighter bite, try Lebkuchen (gingerbread cookies) or Berliner (jam-filled doughnuts), which are often sold at street stalls during festivals.

Food Festivals

Germany is famous for its food festivals, where you can taste regional delicacies, enjoy local drinks, and experience the country's rich culinary heritage. Notable food festivals include:

1. Oktoberfest (Munich): The world's largest beer festival, where you can sample traditional Bavarian food and wash it down with authentic German beers.

2. Christmas Markets (Across Germany): A festive celebration of German culture featuring a variety of delights such as mulled wine (Glühwein), gingerbread cookies, roasted chestnuts, and traditional sausages.

3. Fischmarkt (Hamburg): Held every Sunday, this market is a great place to try fresh seafood and local snacks.

How to Enjoy Local Food Experiences While on a Road Trip

When traveling by car, be sure to stop at local Biergärten (beer gardens), Gaststätten (traditional inns), and local markets to savor authentic German cuisine. Many rural towns host festivals celebrating their culinary specialties; attending these events provides an intimate and authentic food experience.

Beyond the Tourist Trail

Avoid the major tourist hubs when seeking culinary adventures. The best experiences often lie slightly off the beaten path. Look for smaller towns and villages, where local markets might be buzzing with fresh produce, meats, and cheeses. These are your best bet for authentically experiencing the local food scene.

This section serves as a starting point for your exploration of Germany's accommodation options.

The Ritz-Carlton, Berlin

InterContinental berlin

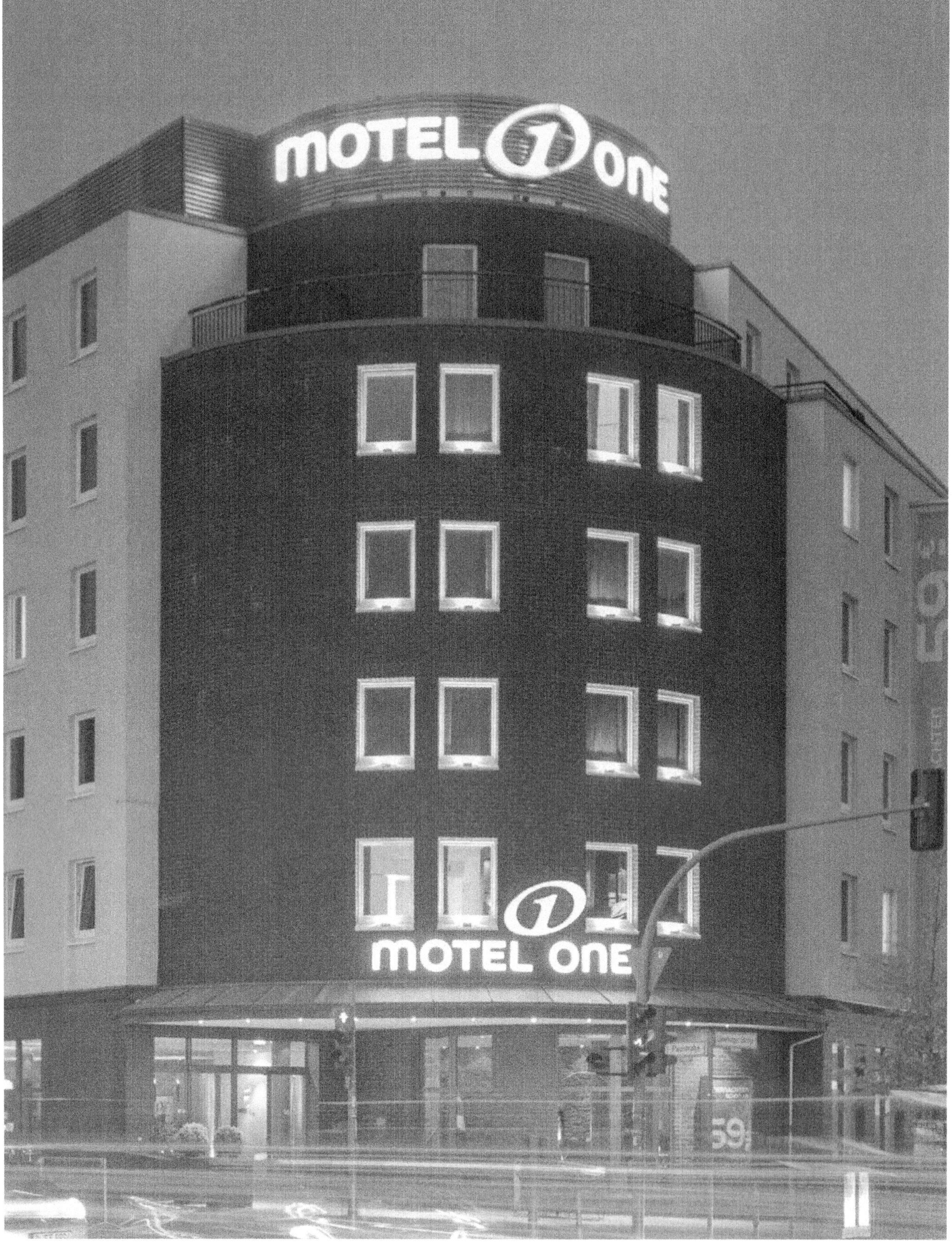
MOTEL ONE
MOTEL ONE

B&B Hotel

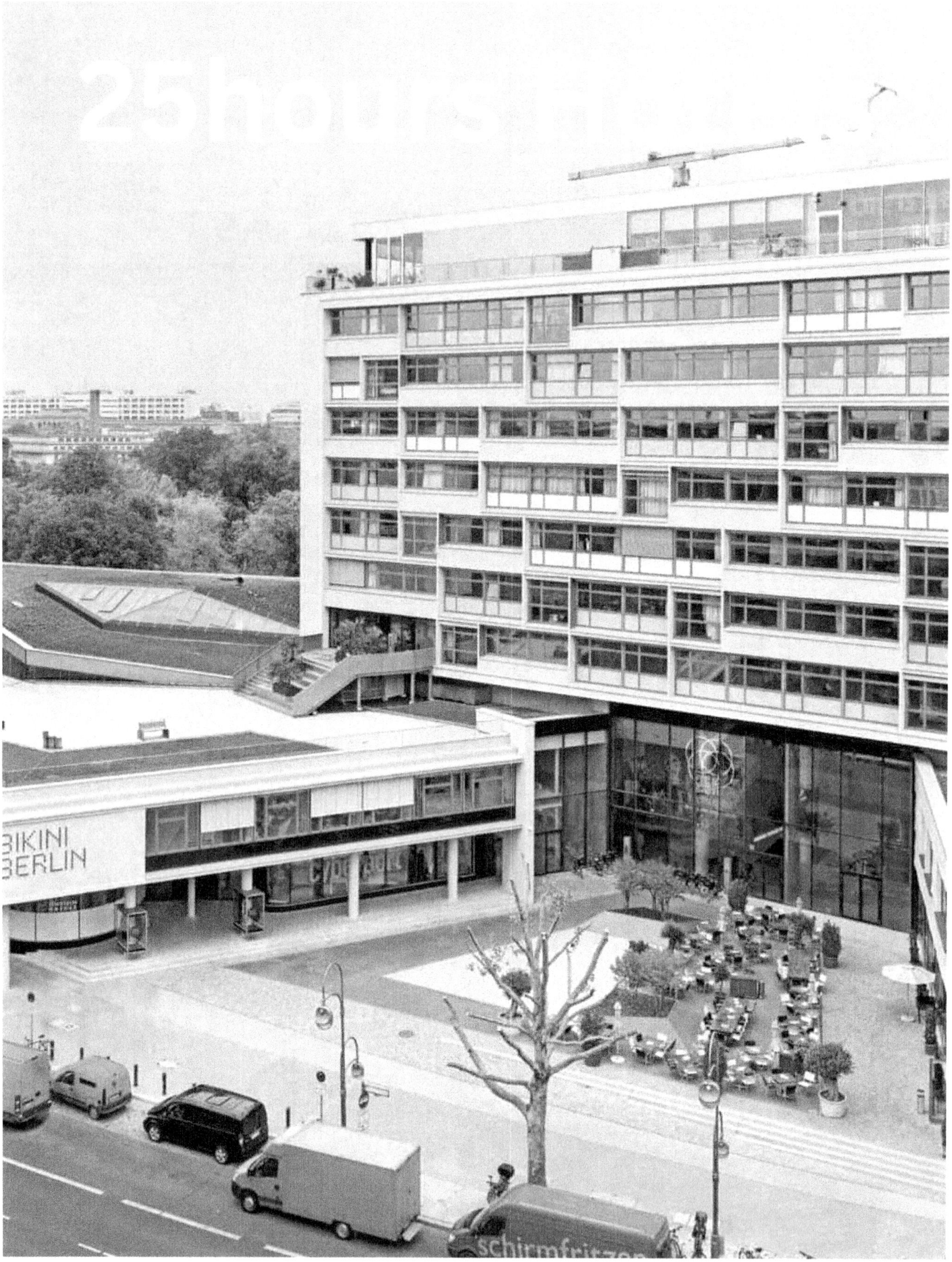
25hours
BIKINI
BERLIN
schirmfritzen

Black Forest

Rhine Valley

The Circus Hostel

A&O Hostel

EastSeven Berlin Hostel

Curry Rico

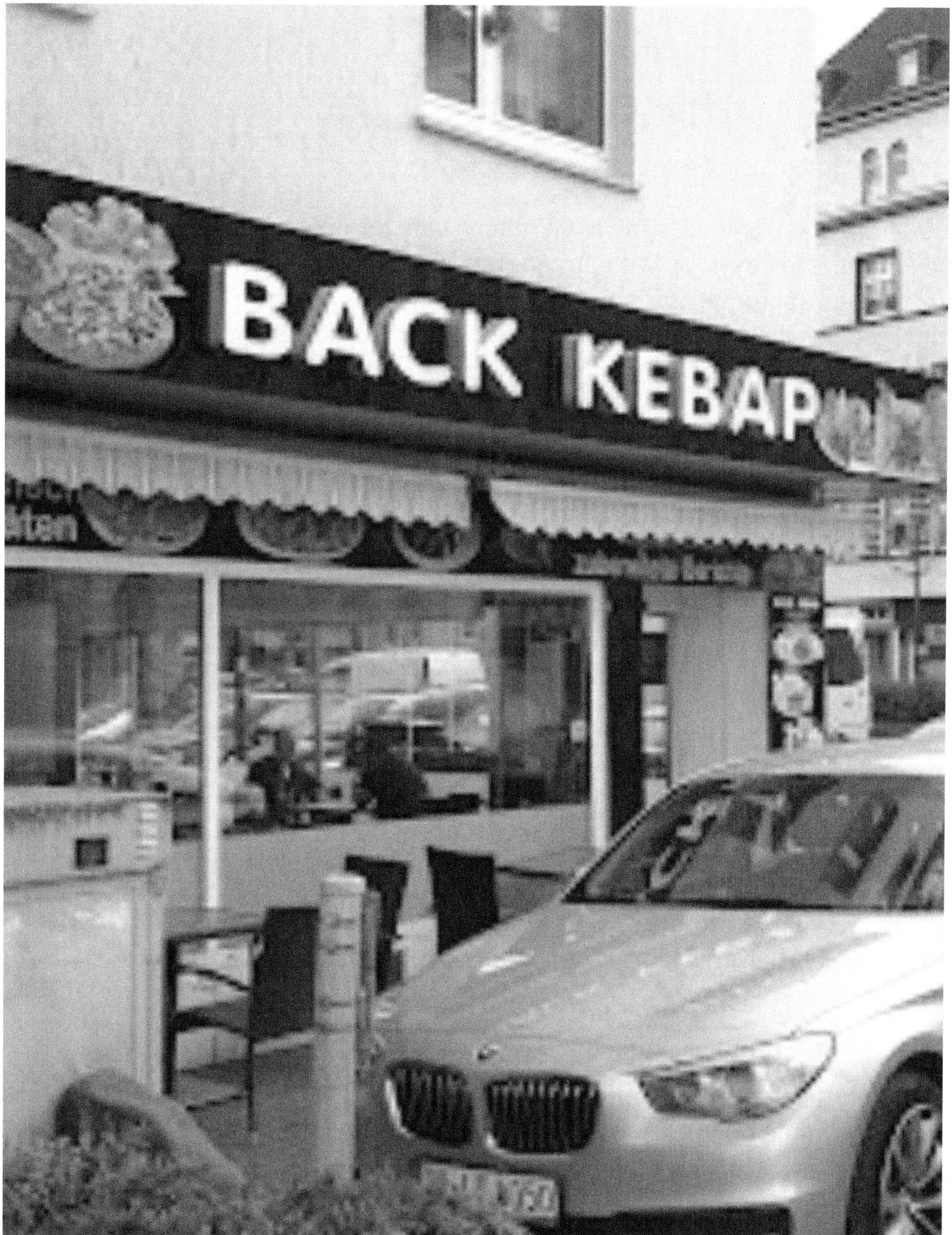
BACK KEBAP

Chapter 8

Final Tips for a Safe and Enjoyable Road Trip

Embarking on a road trip in Germany can be an exciting and memorable adventure. However, as with any journey, prioritizing safety is essential. Here are some important safety tips and guidelines to help you handle any emergencies that may arise on the road.

Road Trip Safety

How to Handle Emergencies on the Road (Accidents, Breakdowns)

Accidents and breakdowns are unpredictable, but being prepared can significantly reduce stress when they happen. First and foremost, ensure you have a roadside emergency kit. This should include basic tools, a flashlight, a warning triangle, first-aid supplies, and essential contact numbers (your car rental company, insurance, and roadside assistance).

In the case of a breakdown, immediately pull over to a safe location. On the autobahn, if your car is still operational, aim for an emergency lane, but always be aware of fast-moving vehicles. Turn on your hazard lights and place the warning triangle at least 100 meters behind the car.

For accidents, German law requires you to report any incident involving injuries or significant damage to the police. If the crash is minor, you can move the vehicles to a safe spot. If you're renting a car, contact your Rental Company and insurance provider immediately to understand the next steps for handling the situation.

Emergency Numbers and Roadside Assistance Services

Germany has excellent emergency services, and knowing the right numbers can save valuable time. In case of an emergency, dial 112 for fire and medical emergencies and 110 for the police.

Many car rental companies in Germany offer roadside assistance services, and they can help with flat tires, battery issues, or other mechanical failures. Make sure you have the contact information for your rental agency and any roadside assistance service provided.

Insurance and Safety Checks

Before hitting the road, ensure that you're properly covered by car insurance. If you're renting a car, double-check the details of your insurance policy. Many companies offer options for roadside assistance as part of their service. Ensure you also know the emergency repair services included, whether it's a simple tire change or more complicated mechanical assistance.

Travel Etiquette

When you're on the road, it's not just about reaching your destination it's about enjoying the journey and respecting local traditions. Here's how to maintain good travel etiquette on the road.

How to Behave on the Road and in Rest Areas

German drivers are known for their efficiency and adherence to traffic laws. Respecting the flow of traffic and driving courteously will help ensure a smooth and enjoyable experience.

When stopping at rest areas (Autohöfe), be considerate of other travelers. Avoid parking in spaces designated for larger vehicles or trucks unless necessary. If you're in a car, try to park in spots designated for smaller cars to allow larger vehicles enough space.

It's also customary to clean up after yourself at rest stops. Dispose of trash properly and leave rest areas as you found them. Public spaces, especially in natural settings, should be treated to preserve the beauty and cleanliness of the country.

Respecting the Environment and Local Traditions

German culture places great emphasis on environmental consciousness and sustainability. It's important to respect this ethos during your road trip. For example, avoid littering or leaving waste behind at scenic spots. Dispose of recyclable materials in designated bins, and whenever possible, choose eco-friendly travel practices.

In rural areas, driving at a moderate speed not only ensures safety but also helps reduce environmental impact. In some rural regions, you might encounter farm vehicles or cyclists, so always be mindful and patient on the road.

Sustainability on the Road

One of the best ways to enhance your road trip experience while minimizing environmental impact is by embracing sustainable travel practices.

Eco-friendly Travel Habits for Reducing Your Carbon Footprint

Germany is a leader in promoting sustainability, and there are many ways to reduce your environmental impact while traveling. If you have the option, consider driving a hybrid or electric vehicle, which significantly lowers carbon emissions. Many rental companies offer these options, and Germany has an extensive network of charging stations across the country.

Additionally, practice fuel-efficient driving techniques, such as maintaining a steady speed, using cruise control where possible, and reducing unnecessary idling. These simple practices can help you minimize fuel consumption and contribute to a greener trip.

Green Accommodations and Sustainable Road Trip Options

As you plan your stops along the way, look for eco-friendly accommodations. Many hotels, guesthouses, and campsites in Germany are committed to sustainability, offering green certifications and environmentally friendly amenities. Some even feature solar panels, energy-efficient appliances, and water-saving measures.

Along your route, you may also encounter restaurants, wineries, and farms that prioritize local, organic food.

Service Areas on the Autobahn

The German autobahn is known for its efficiency and quality, and the service areas along these highways are an integral part of the driving experience. These rest stops, called Autohöfe, are equipped with everything travelers need to relax, refuel, and take a break from their journey.

What to Expect at German Highway Rest Stops (Autohöfe)

Autohöfe are well-maintained and offer a variety of services, making them perfect for a quick pit stop. You'll find gas stations, fast food restaurants, coffee shops, and even sit-down dining options. Some rest stops also have supermarkets, where you can grab snacks, drinks, or essentials you may have forgotten. These facilities are conveniently located at regular intervals along the autobahn, ensuring you won't have to travel too far before finding a spot to rest.

Many Autohöfe also offer clean restrooms, baby-changing facilities, and pet areas. For longer stops, some of these rest areas even have small hotels or guesthouses where you can get some rest before continuing your journey.

Best Places for Food, Coffee, and Rest Along Major Routes

Along Germany's autobahns, certain rest stops stand out for their exceptional services and food offerings. Some popular Autohöfe, such as those on the A1 between Cologne and Hamburg or the A5 between Frankfurt and Karlsruhe, offer excellent local fare like bratwurst, pretzels, and hearty regional specialties. Whether you're looking for a quick snack or a full meal, these rest areas cater to all needs.

If you're a coffee lover, look out for rest stops with specialty cafes, often serving freshly brewed coffee and pastries. This is the perfect way to recharge before continuing your drive.

Convenient Facilities like Gas Stations, Showers, and Wi-Fi

The autobahn's rest stops are equipped with convenient facilities to make your journey as comfortable as possible. You can refuel both your car and yourself with easy access to gas stations and food outlets. Some larger Autohöfe even have shower facilities, allowing you to freshen up if you're on a long drive or road trip.

Many rest areas also provide free or paid Wi-Fi, allowing you to stay connected, check your route, or even book accommodations for your next stop.

Scenic Stops and Hidden Gems

While the autobahn is known for its efficiency, Germany is filled with scenic stops and hidden gems that are well worth the detour. Here are some suggestions for making your road trip even more memorable.

Historic Sites and Monuments Along the Roads

Germany is home to numerous historic sites, castles, and monuments, many of which are conveniently located just off the major highways. Whether it's the majestic Heidelberg Castle or the historic Sanssouci Palace in Potsdam, these sites are perfect for a short visit during your road trip.

Charming Villages and Towns Perfect for a Stopover

While you're on the road, take the time to explore some of the charming towns and villages that Germany is known for. Villages such as Rothenburg ob der Tauber, along the Romantic Road, or the picturesque Gengenbach in the Black Forest offer a glimpse of traditional German life and culture. These spots are often less crowded than the major cities but offer just as much charm and history.

Nature Reserves and Hiking Spots Close to Highways

Germany's highways are often surrounded by breathtaking natural landscapes, with many national parks, nature reserves, and hiking trails just a short drive away. If you have the time, stop at places like the Bavarian Forest or the Eifel National Park, where you can hike, take in panoramic views, and enjoy the tranquility of nature.

By integrating these scenic stops into your itinerary, you can experience the full beauty of Germany while traveling by road.

Heidelberg Castle

Sanssouci Palace

Gengenbach

Bavarian Forest

Nationalpark Eifel

Chapter 9

Conclusion

Final Reflections, Road Wisdom & Travel Takeaways

As your journey through this guidebook draws to a close, what begins is your personal adventure through one of Europe's most captivating and culturally rich nations: Germany. You've now packed a wealth of information into your travel toolkit: maps, routes, cultural insights, and region-specific highlights all tailored to make your experience not just successful but truly memorable.

Whether you're planning a solo exploration, a family vacation, a romantic getaway, or an immersive dive into history, food, and nature, this guide was built with you in mind: the curious traveler, the responsible adventurer, the one who wants to experience Germany rather than just see it.

So let's recap the most vital points, share a few final thoughts, and leave you inspired and ready for the road ahead.

A Recap of Your Road Trip Playbook

Planning Like a Pro

From the first chapter, we talked extensively about preparation. Not the kind that makes you overpack and overthink, but the kind that ensures your documents, gear, apps, and knowledge are right where they should be. In 2025, travel to Germany is smoother than ever, but it still pays to be ready:

Passport and visa rules? Sorted.

Travel insurance? Covered.

Car rental documents and international driving permits? Handled.

You've got the Euro currency tips, mobile payments setup, and all the details about credit cards and ATM use. You know how to pack light if you're hopping between cities and what to bring if you're camping under the stars in Bavaria or cruising down the Rhine.

Mastering the Roads

Once you hit the road, you're navigating with confidence. Germany's roads are among the best-maintained in Europe, and with our guidance on Autobahns, Bundesstraßen, and city driving nuances, you're no longer a tourist-you're a road-tripper who blends in.

You understand

- The differences between city and countryside driving
- How to read road signs and speed limits (and when there aren't any)
- Where to park, how to refuel, and how to stay safe in winter conditions

From handling roundabouts like a local to respecting Umweltzones with the right emissions sticker, your knowledge isn't just surface-level-it's practical and current.

Discovering the Regions

In Chapter 3, we peeled back the curtain on each corner of Germany:

The seafront charm of the North-think Lübeck's old town, breezy Baltic beaches, and the maritime elegance of Hamburg.

The storybook landscapes of the South, with castles, forests, and Alpine beauty that feel ripped from a fairytale.

The vibrant culture of East Berlin dynamic energy, Dresden refined elegance, and Leipzig's thriving creativity.

The classic charm of the West wine routes, Roman relics, and riverside towns full of warmth and character.

This is not just geography. It's a tapestry of dialects, flavors, and traditions that change every couple of hours on the road.

Choosing the Best Routes

Germany is designed for road trips. We've equipped you with multiple themed routes:

Romantic Road? Check.

Fairy Tale Route? Ready.

Castle Road, Wine Route, or the Black Forest High Road? You've got maps, highlights, and insider tips.

Highways, Networks, and Tools

From apps like Google Maps and Waze to good old paper atlases, you now know how to plan and adapt in real time. Whether you're avoiding traffic jams or looking for hidden gems en route, you're in full control of your travel narrative.

Final Travel Etiquette & Safety Tips

Germany is modern and well-organized, but being a mindful traveler always pays off.

Use rest areas and Autohöfe to recharge-respect cleanliness rules and public spaces.

Don't forget pedestrian zones-parking improperly here can result in fines.

Exercise patience with local customs, particularly when dining or dealing with administrative procedures.

In emergencies, dial 112. Germany's emergency services are efficient and multilingual, especially in urban areas. Keep your health insurance card, roadside assistance number, and emergency contact info handy in both physical and digital formats.

Sustainable Road Travel

Your journey should leave memories, not a trail of pollution. You've read about:

Renting or driving electric and hybrid vehicles

Finding charging stations

Choosing eco-friendly accommodations

Reducing waste during your journey

These aren't just travel tips; they're ways of protecting the natural beauty of Germany for future generations of road-trippers.

Where to Sleep, What to Eat

Germany offers a diverse array of accommodation options to suit every traveler's style and budget. From historic inns nestled in charming towns to modern hotels in bustling cities, the country ensures a comfortable stay whether you're seeking luxury or budget-friendly options.

Germany offers

- Quirky guesthouses run by local families
- Campsites that blend with nature
- Hostels in historic buildings and urban centers
- Michelin-starred restaurants and curbside sausage stalls

Remember the names: schnitzel, currywurst, spätzle, käsespätzle, döner kebab, Maultaschen, Weißwurst, Apfelstrudel. They aren't just food they're fuel for your journey and your memory bank.

Plan around food festivals, farmers markets, and regional specialties to get the most out of every bite.

Beyond the Road: Hidden Corners worth Exploring

Don't overlook

Small towns like Quedlinburg, Meersburg, or Rothenburg ob der Tauber

Natural wonders like Saxon Switzerland, the Berchtesgaden Alps, or the Eifel Volcano region

Historical spots not on the mainstream tourist trail

Some of the most soul-stirring moments of your trip won't be from places on a list. They'll come unexpectedly like a detour through a foggy forest road, a morning coffee in a sleepy village square, or a conversation with a baker in a tiny town you've never heard of.

Final Words of Encouragement

Let's be honest: no guidebook can ever fully prepare you for the emotions of the journey-the thrill of discovery, the peaceful silence of a sunrise drive, or the laughter echoing off castle walls. However, the right guide can instill confidence and help you make the most of your adventure. Let the detailed maps and informative entries spark your curiosity, inspiring you to plan your next exploration. Embrace the spirit of discovery, and may your travels through Germany in 2025 be filled with unforgettable experiences.

That's what we've done here.

You're not just "traveling through Germany." You're building a story, one road sign at a time. You're navigating more than highways; you're crossing cultural bridges, tasting heritage, and hearing history speak through the landscape.

Final Travel Checklist

Before you hit the road, make sure you've got:

- Valid passport, visa, and international driver's permit
- Insurance (travel and car)
- Navigation tools (offline & online)
- Environmental sticker for city access
- Winter tires or chains (depending on the season)
- Emergency roadside kit
- Local currency and digital payment options
- Accommodation confirmations
- Language guide or translation app
- A playlist or podcast lineup for the road

A Note from the Author

Every kilometer you travel adds a chapter to your personal story. I hope this guide helps you write it with confidence, safety, and wonder.

So, pack your bags—light or heavy, your choice. Turn the key, roll the windows down, and hit the road.

Happy family

Printed in Dunstable, United Kingdom